Also by Karen Benke

Poetry
Sister

Creative Nonfiction
Rip the Page!
Leap Write In!

Write Back Soon!

ADVENTURES IN Letter WRITING

KAREN BENKE

ROOST BOOKS
BOSTON AND LONDON
2015

Roost Books
An imprint of Shambhala Publications, Inc.
Horticultural Hall
300 Massachusetts Avenue
Boston, Massachusetts 02115
roostbooks.com

Pages 197–99 constitute a continuation of the copyright page.

First Edition
Printed in the United States of America

⊗ This edition is printed on acid-free paper that meets the American National
Standards Institute Z39.48 Standard.
♻ Shambhala Publications makes every effort to print on recycled paper.
For more information please visit www.shambhala.com.

Distributed in the United States by Penguin Random House LLC and
in Canada by Random House of Canada Ltd

Designed by Allison Meierding

Library of Congress Cataloging-in-Publication Data

Benke, Karen.
Write back soon!: adventures in letter writing/Karen Benke.—First edition.
    pages cm
Includes bibliographical references and index.
ISBN 978-1-61180-268-9 (pbk.: alk. paper)
1. Letter writing. 2. Authorship. 3. English language—Composition and
exercises. I. Title.
PE1483.B46 2015
808.6—dc23
2014045471

For Lynn—pal with the coolest pens, forever-friend

Only write to me, write to me,
I love to see the hop and skip and sudden starts of your ink.

—A. S. Byatt, *Possession*

Contents

Write Back Soon! is for anyone—friends, family members, acquaintances, students—who may have forgotten they like to play with the way a pen rides the surface of paper, to create words that tumble and flow into a note or letter. It's for people who enjoy writing by hand, penning an address, selecting stamps, and seeing those wavy cancellation lines and that official postmark in the upper right-hand corner of an envelope. It's for *all* lovers of snail mail—both senders and receivers. Mostly, though, it's for those near and far with whom we want to stay in touch via a postcard, note, package, or letter that shares our essence via handwriting.

Uncapping a pen to write to a friend can calm us down; lift us up; and connect us to a treasured someone a few blocks over, in the next city or state, in another country, or an ocean away. The words we form by holding a pen are different from those we create by pressing plastic keys and staring at a screen. E-mails may have instant impact, but letters have *lasting* impact. A handwritten letter, with its one-of-a-kind look and style, can be returned to and appreciated again and again. The giving of a note or letter is a tactile gift for both giver and receiver, since the letters we write offer a way to share feelings and observations that are often more intimate than our speech allows us to reveal. The letters we send can also be more trans-formative than those we receive, as it's during the formation of a letter and in the waiting for a response that we feel the wonder, anticipation, and ultimately the joy that our words are going to be "met" by a friend.

Like you, I own a computer and use it to communicate, pushing those ubiquitous square buttons while looking at a backlit screen. In fact, I'm doing it right now as I write to you, although I did first create *Write Back Soon!* using a favorite black pen and multiple sheets of paper. When I want to connect with a special friend, e-mailing and texting provide a much less satisfying experience, not to mention sore thumbs and wrists, a slouched back, and hunched shoulders. Who needs more of *that*? Besides, people often delete or save an e-mail exchange but rarely return to it. An electronic message leaves me feeling less connection and warmth than an actual letter that has been touched by a friend's hands and is now in my hands—or was touched by *my* hands and is now living with a friend. Bottom line: I adore the smudges, cross-outs, doodles, and underlines of a letter.

Some of us have gotten so attached to shooting off that abbreviated lowercase text and sending out a quick e-mail that we've completely forgotten about the simple and satisfying act of this slower form of communication that's always available to us: sitting down to pen a friendly "Hi, how are you? I'm thinking of you today" in a note that tells someone, "You're important to me. I believe in you." I get that our device-driven style of communication isn't going away anytime soon, and I don't know that I'd want it to, but I do wonder if we can incorporate other modes of slow communication back into our repertoires again. Can we live with delayed gratification and expectation for a few days rather than constantly checking to see who has just sent us a message and instantly firing off a response? Handwritten words sealed in an envelope that we mail to a friend, or that a friend has taken the time to create and send to us, can bring a rush of comfort and a surge of happiness that feels like a hug from afar. And we all need more of *that*.

Write Back Soon! is a collection of note-passing and letter-writing ideas to make you a better correspondent. It's a collection of hints to stimulate your imagination about what to write and who to write to, with a multitude of ideas to get you back in the habit of connecting by hand. Many of the prompts in *Write Back Soon!* suggest you pen something the size of a postcard. Easy. Many of the letter lead-ins are simply examples of beginnings that can help you bridge the gap to a middle. I contacted some of my favorite writers to ask them to share with you why they like to write by hand and, more specifically, what penning notes and letters means to them. You'll find these in "A Note Passed to You" sections. Word lists are handy if you're at a loss for what rhymes with *postmark*, say, or are in need of just the right adjective. Other sections contain little-known facts about the U.S. mail and zip codes and how writing by hand corresponds with a calm and focused mind. This book can be opened to any page to inspire the letter writer in you to begin to consider and connect, via paper and pen, with patience and imagination. It includes that short field trip to the big blue mailbox, pulling down the metal handle, dropping your letter inside, and then enjoying the anticipation. On the other end of this gift is the recipient, peering into the cavelike space of his mailbox, where you are waiting in the form of your words, stories, and news on paper. Surprise, excitement, memory, emotion—all passed along by myriad hands—have arrived! What a lift! Now you, too, have an opportunity to write back soon.

Love,
Karen

P.S. You might even mail someone this book and include a little "hint, hint" note along with it.

Send It in Seventeen Syllables

Most of us are way too busy with our seemingly endless to-do lists, which may be why we often write in abbreviated "nglsh" and sound bites. But seeing a word written out is beautiful, a sign that someone has taken time and cares enough for herself and for us to slow life down a notch or two. A complete thought or sentence is, in a word, refreshing. If you want to try out something new to give away later, carve out a seventeen-minute break in your day and check out the American haiku: one sentence of exactly seventeen syllables that was created by the poet Allen Ginsberg. Use this easy form to share a part of your day or some insight with a friend nearby or far away. Or with seventeen friends. After all, this is what friends do—we tell each other stuff.

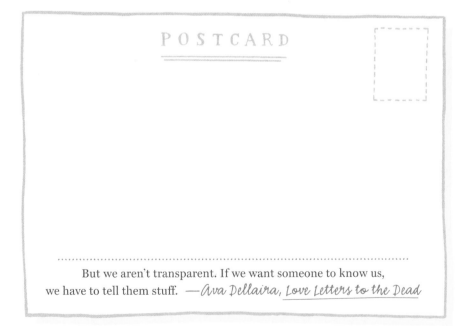

P O S T C A R D

But we aren't transparent. If we want someone to know us,
we have to tell them stuff. —*Ava Dellaira, Love Letters to the Dead*

A Hello the Length of a Line

E. M. Forster said, "Letters have to pass two tests before they can be classified as good: they must express the personality both of the writer and of the recipient." I've found that some of the shortest notes I've received pass Forster's two tests. My mother likes to send small nonbossy reminders: "Have your best day ever, Katrina." Or this note, received years ago and found today tucked between the pages of a poetry book: "Slow down, sweet girl, it's only to yourself that you're moving." She sends her signature homemade cookies, individually wrapped in tinfoil and packed in shoeboxes, to family and friends with her recipe-messages: "Not too much sugar but a whole lot of love."

My father practiced the art of calligraphy and left notes in unique places. Once, when he was painting our house, he labelled an entire section—the length of the street-facing living room wall—with "K-a-r-i-e," to show me where I could help him cover up the old yellow with the new green. Other times, he left notes in the margins of my *Merriam-Webster's Student Dictionary* next to certain words such as *love, writer, daughter.*

My nana painted small watercolors on squares of recycled cardboard—lopsided pumpkins, pink roses from her garden—and included a five-dollar bill with instructions to "Treat yourself to an ice cream cone, Dolly!"

LETTER LEAD-IN

Send a short letter to someone in your family and let it express something unique about your personality. It can be as easy as describing where you're sitting: "Hi, I'm at Poets House in New York City at a table by the window, looking out at the Hudson River, thinking of you. . . ." May you feel the world grow closer, cozier, and friendlier with this gesture.

So Much to Be Done

So much gets in the way of sitting down to write a letter to a friend, my sister, even my former mother-in-law, whom I adore and who writes the loveliest letters back. I want to pen a response to my editor for the thoughtful book she sent and find a stamp for that congratulations card sitting on the entry table so it will reach the son of a friend who is graduating from college soon. But there are dishes to wash, paw prints on the windowsill, Cheerios stuck in the heater grate (Who did that?)—tiny unkept altars that always need neatening no matter how much I sweep and weed, dust and fold.

Ignoring these distractions I take a pen from the glass jar on my desk and, in the middle of yet another domestic mess, pull cat Clive close and sit on the sunny side of the window seat. I remind myself that each moment is always right here, always perfect, before it fades and another takes its place.

My son, no longer a child, sits on the couch with a science book open in his lap and explains, "We're all made of atoms and light. Everything's empty space, Mom." I look up from my letter and consider Clive's white fur, a wilted flower, sand on the cushions courtesy of new dog Rasco Roon. My son wanders into the kitchen to pour himself a bowl of Rice Krispies and asks if I want anything. We swallow spoonfuls of swirling protons, orbiting electrons. He crumples up another piece of paper and worries over a test. I confess I don't understand his homework, though I know for a fact it's love that binds the zigzags of time to his expanding life and mine.

Shooting me a smile I've loved all his life, he returns to reading, high-lighting, taking notes, while I continue to pen my letter, sharing with a friend a country away this slice of time spent with the cat, the dog, and my son, never mind the dishes and the laundry. The chores can wait.

LETTER LEAD-IN

A handwritten letter is a creative act. Start your next letter with, "Though there's much to be done," and list a few of the chores that occupy your day. Often it's news of the mundane that brings us the most pleasure while reading a letter. Don't let it sit longer than a day. Find that stamp and mail it.

Dear Reader,

What I practice is availability. That is a practice. It doesn't mean that I am not doing other things, but I am aware that I should stop doing whatever I am doing when something like a poem begins to sneak up on me.

g.s.

A SAMPLE OF GARY SNYDER'S WRITING
From *Distant Neighbors*

Wendell—

Glad you weren't blown away (or your barns) in the recent tornados —and thanks for the poems. —I'm sure you'll be out this way some-time—of course no rush, so much work here, too (and mountain weather—a sudden snowfall right now—big flakes).
best,

gary

GARY SNYDER lives on his homestead in the Sierra Foothills and is a neighbor and community activist in the Yuba River Watershed. He has written more than twenty works of prose and poetry that explore connections among ecology, Eastern philosophy, and indigenous anthropology. He and writer Wendell Berry have exchanged letters since the early 1970s, many of which can be read in *Distant Neighbors: The Selected Letters of Wendell Berry and Gary Snyder.*

Giving a Gift on Your Birthday

No matter how old you get, completing another turn around the sun can still be exciting—with the good wishes and cards, the phone calls and greetings, the cake and all those candles. While birthdays can get pretty elaborate, which I love, I also appreciate the Japanese tradition of a gift being given with both hands and the custom of opening birthday presents in private. I read recently about how the Japanese say, *"Tsumaranai mono desu ga,"* which means "This is a trivial thing, but please accept it," when giving a gift. This statement conveys that the relationship is more important than the gift. Of course, we can agree that people are more important than things, but it's also fun to wrap gifty things up and give them away, especially things made by an artist (you) and presented to someone who will truly appreciate them. If you were to give someone a gift on *your* birthday, what would it be? It might be a story or a drawing or a loaf of homemade bread. Or perhaps a garland of hearts cut from an old atlas. To whom would you give or send it? You might start the accompanying note with: "Today's my birthday. This is for you."

POSTCARD

There are three hundred and sixty-four days when you might get un-birthday presents, and only one for birthday presents, you know. —*Lewis Carroll*

WHAT YOU CAN SEND THROUGH THE MAIL

No need to put any of the following into a box with brown wrapping, tape, and twine. Simply write the address with a permanent marker *directly on* the object, affix enough postage, and—voilà—that's it. Depending on how much it weighs and where it's going, the U.S. Postal Service will be happy to mail it for you "parcel post" minus any packaging. They do draw the line at children being sent through the mail, however, as one couple in Ohio discovered in 1913 when they paid fifteen cents in stamps, insured their small son for fifty dollars, and tried to mail him off to his grandma. The post office considers everything on the following list a "self-contained object." Not sure if an item you want to send is self-contained? Take a walk to your local post office and ask. While you're at it, check out the selection of stamps.

A potato (Write, "French fries or paperweight?" on it.)

A Frisbee (Write, "Let's meet at the park," on it.)

A disposable camera (Snap a photo first; then write, "Mystery photo enclosed," on the outside.)

A pillow (Write, "Close your eyes and imagine a hug," on it.)

A bucket and shovel (Write, "Wanna go to the beach?" on it.)

A rock (Write, "Skip me far," on it.)

An inflated beach ball (Write, "Let's play," on it.)

A piñata (Fill it with notes and quotes.)

A coconut (Write a riddle about a monkey.)

A box of candy (Write, "Let's meet for a movie.")

A hat for any occasion (Yes, a sombrero is allowed.)

A homing pigeon (See page 14 to find out more.)

A plastic bottle (Put a message inside or fill it with colored pencils.)

P.S. Every year Ripley's Believe It or Not! holds a strange mail contest. Check out past years' submissions on their website (www.ripleys.com /mail) and then get ready to be inspired to send your own brand of something specifically wild and wacky through the mail . . .

LETTER WRITERS ALLIANCE

Founders Donovan and Kathy welcomed me to Letter Writers Alliance (LWA) by sending a handwritten card inside a handwritten envelope complete with cool stamps on the front. The letter, though homemade, also looked official. I tossed aside the bills and ads and sat right down with Rasco Roon on the front porch to examine my new membership card. Rasco, excited for me, licked the card—but, then, his doggy-tongue licks everything.

Donovan and Kathy started Letter Writers Alliance in 2007, because they believe a handwritten letter is a rare and wondrous thing—yes, indeed—and wanted to preserve this art form. It was as simple as that. They, along with all LWA members, myself included (I count myself as member 5,001), promise that "neither long lines, nor late deliveries, nor increasing postal rates will keep us from our mission."

If you love tangible correspondence—and who, I ask, doesn't?—and you'd like to become a card-carrying lifetime member and perhaps find a pen pal, contact Letter Writers Alliance. For $5, you'll receive an official Write More Letters card to carry in your wallet; gain access to a worldwide pen pal swap from England to New Zealand, Australia to Canada; and receive free stationery downloads and a badge to sew onto your favorite writing notebook. Donovan and Kathy are rooting for you to "prepare your pen and paper, moisten your tongue, and get ready to write more letters." Their website is used as the official "club house" hub and provides everything you could possibly need or want, from rubber stamps to postcards, and even a homing pigeon (fake) to tuck a note into.

No excuses: go offline *now*. Step outside with paper and a pen. Write, seal, send!

SOME POSTAGE REQUIRED

Letter Writers Alliance
P.O. Box 221168
Chicago, IL 60622
letterwriters.org

FINDING IMAGES

We walk past a thousand story ideas a day. To see them more easily go in search of some real-life pictures. Or be an extra-aware eavesdropper to find some snappy dialogue. While hiking the Pixie Trail in Mill Valley, California, with my mixed-breed rescue dog who sports a heart-shaped marking on his forehead, I hear myself say, "Rasco Roon, Roonsie-Tune, time to go home, sweet doggy-doo." (I hear other humans call their dogs using affectionate/slightly embarrassing songs too!) Take along a pen and notebook, and capture something that catches your attention mid-moment.

It doesn't matter where you look. Story ideas can be found anywhere from the dog park to the doctor's office ("The nurse drew my blood and *then* asked if I had a history of fainting") to your daily commute ("Driving home: static on the radio mimics fog on the mountain"). Scribble a moment and expand on it later. When later comes, create a few sentences out of your collection. Document where your observations came from. "At the corner of Miller and Evergreen, we hold hands, look both ways, cross to the other side." Send one image via a postcard to a friend.

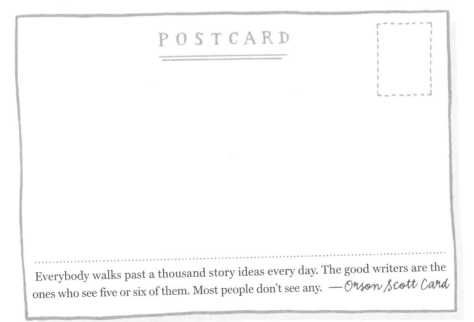

POSTCARD

Everybody walks past a thousand story ideas every day. The good writers are the ones who see five or six of them. Most people don't see any. —*Orson Scott Card*

SOMETHING SHARED

After our father died, my sister, Ali, and I exchanged a photograph of him taken on his fishing boat. He's caught in profile somewhere along the Sacramento River, wind blowing through his thick brown hair. He's wearing a white collared shirt and suspenders and a watch on his wrist. It's a photograph we both love, so I'd keep it for a few months before hand-delivering it or sending it wrapped in several yards of bubble wrap through the mail back to her. This went on for years. We'd correspond via this photograph, tucking in other photos from our childhood—"Nice hair-do, Kares!" Sometimes we'd include a favorite shirt or necklace or pair of socks, specifying "gift" or "loan." Other times, we'd write to tell of a "Dad dream" we'd had: "A drop in altitude, then palm trees—the four of us at an outdoor buffet—saltwater, scent of sunscreen, Dad's arms pulling us close."

I think our father would like knowing how many years and how many miles that photograph traveled between us, how he was a part of our clothing swaps that no longer turned into arguments. Last year, my brother-in-law took that photo of our father out of its wood frame and had a copy made. He sent me an e-mail with the scan and an explanation that it was time Ali and I each had our own copy. While I appreciated his gesture, and my sister did too, it also represented an end to something that was laced with tradition. Now that image of our father, looking off into a distance that neither of us can see, is hanging on two walls in two houses while everything he meant to us, individually and collectively, remains in our hearts. Although I don't yet know what it will be, my sister and I now have the opportunity to start a new tradition of sending something shared through the mail.

LETTER LEAD-IN

Find something irreplaceable that you don't wish to give away but would like to share with someone close to you—a piece of art, a necklace, an article of clothing, even a beloved photograph that you're willing to part with for a few months at a time. Send this, along with a note, to your sister, cousin, or friend, detailing what it means to you.

Sixty-Five Opportunities for More Light

Let's say we have sixty-five chances—a random number—every day to stop and dash off a note of appreciation. Now let's say that these opportunities have the potential to reorient our lives and the lives of other people, to lift us into more light. We're not talking about a fancy-schmancy kind of note on personalized stationery but about something humble, written on whatever's handy, and left where a certain someone can happen upon it—on a paper bag, say, taped to the refrigerator. Perhaps you could make it a short apology for eating the strawberries that were being saved for breakfast, like William Carlos Williams did after he ate those plums made famous from his poem "This Is Just to Say." Or leave a "love ticket" tucked under a friend's windshield wiper to express a quick sentiment of affection or gratitude. You have sixty-five chances to notice, thank, appreciate, explain, share, or apologize for just about anything—"Hey, you oiled the squeaky door to the mudroom. Thanks!" "Heard you sneeze. Elderberry syrup on kitchen table, XO." Finding a reason to leave someone a short note may very well change your and someone else's entire day. Reflect back. Pull out something specific someone did, said, or helped with that made your life easier, brighter, more hopeful. Tell that person in a few words with a favorite pen. Any color will do.

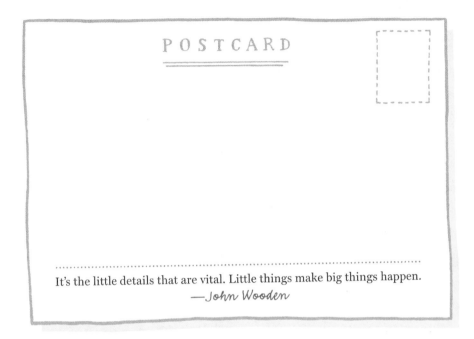

It's the little details that are vital. Little things make big things happen.
—*John Wooden*

Arrive Late, Leave Early

When my sister and I were growing up, our mother was working on her graduate degree in psychology. She did this while helping our nana run a retail business—a maternity shop—on the weekends, interning part-time as a counselor after school, and volunteering for a crisis hotline once we went to bed. Despite how *very* busy she was, she managed to find time to sew costumes for my dance recitals; drive my sister to her swim meets; and take the two of us for girls-only shopping trips, movie outings, and special lunches.

We'd slide into a booth at TGI Friday's with our shopping bags and look through the menu. Waiting for our lunch to arrive, our mother would lean in and whisper, "Okay, see that guy over there? That's my boyfriend, Hector. He's pretending he doesn't notice me." My sister and I would casually look over at a man minding his own business, eating a sandwich. It was a game we played. My mother would start in the middle of the story, with my sister and I adding on. "Just look at him—he's hopelessly in love with me but can't bring himself to say it," our mother would insist. "He lost his job this morning. His supervisor had it in for him," my sister continued. "Poor guy." "But, it's okay," I'd tack on, "because now he can visit his brother and sister-in-law in Salt Lake City and get to know his nephew better." Over dessert, we'd plan the remaining years of Hector's life. "He'll meet his future wife on that flight to Utah and commit to finally finishing his novel," our mother started again. "But, wait, what about you, Mom?" my sister asked, confused. "Isn't Hector *your* boyfriend?" Endings can be confusing, no matter if they're real or made up.

LETTER LEAD-IN

The next time you're having lunch with your mother, sister, or friend, find a character like Hector and start making up your own story about that person. Give yourself the gift of time, and write it down.

Pushing Words toward Each Other

Poets William Stafford and Marvin Bell met in 1979 at the Midnight Sun Visiting Writers Series at the University of Alaska in Fairbanks. Stafford was from Washington; Bell was from Iowa. After the conference, they decided to keep in touch. But how? Being poets—and teachers—they hit on the idea of sending poems back and forth. For the next two years, their friendship took shape from that decision "to push words toward each other" in a total of twenty-two poems apiece. Their poems-as-letters were eventually bound into a collection called *Segues: A Correspondence in Poetry.* (*Segues* is a term for the transitions inside a piece of music that allow one theme to grow into another.)

April and Bruce met five years ago at a Society of Children's Book Writers and Illustrators conference; they now send each other a poem a day via "sail-mail," since Bruce lives on a boat and travels around the world. If the muse arrives late, they use the code PHP for placeholder poem, for any poem that had to be dashed out in a hurry. They often build off the subjects of each other's poems and segue into what's going on in their lives via their postscripts—"The sail tore"; "Just arrived in Guam"; "The dog got sick"; "Out-of-town guests . . . baking lasagna for dinner."

Find someone to correspond with. Pick someone with whom you'd like to see a friendship evolve. Make a pact to exchange poems as letters over a certain amount of time. Let the subject matter of a received letter-poem inspire you when you write back. This kind of relationship creates intimacy. Try it. You'll see.

POSTCARD

Friendship is born at that moment when one person says to another:
What! You, too? I thought I was the only one.   —C. S. Lewis

Greetings and Good-byes

There are so many ways to start and sign off on a letter. Here are some of the most typical, tried and true. Plus some you may never have dreamt of using. And a few you might laugh at, but give a try anyway the next time you open and close a letter to an adventurous friend or family member.

GREETINGS

Good day

Hi

Hello

Dear

Salutations

Oh, Pal of Mine

Hey, this is your moment

Salut (if you're feeling French)

OPENING LINES AFTER YOUR GREETING

You've always been there for me . . .

Although we haven't talked as much as we used to, . . .

Friends like you are the reason why I'm able to . . .

GOOD-BYES

Love always

Later Alligator

Till next time

Hugs

Cheers

With a smile

With inspiration

I miss you

Rooting for you

You're the best

Double blessings

Ciao (if you're feeling Italian)

Catch Some Dialogue

"I'm so tired of seeing him on that device," a man muttered to his wife. I was eating lunch in front of my friend Saru's Punjabi burrito café, but on hearing this, I sensed a story-scene unfolding and reached for my pen. The family of three was trudging in a little line up Madrona Street. Between sips of a mango lassi, I caught bits of their conversation. The screen-user straggled behind his parents, head down, fingers flying over tiny keys. "I say ban those things," a woman at the next table whispered to her companion. Her friend nodded, then checked her cell phone. The screen-user's mother instructed in a sharp tone, "Daniel, turn that thing off, or it goes away." His father observed, "Look, he can't even hear you."

The author of *Get Shorty*, Elmore Leonard, once said, "All the information you need can be given in dialogue." Tune in to a conversation going on near you. One that makes you smile. Or frown. Catch a few or a few hundred words that bombard your ears via dialogue—a conversation you can retell, expand on paper, and share with a friend later.

POSTCARD

Dialogue is a little bit jazz, a little bit hand-to-hand combat.
—Chuck Wendig

WRITING ON SCRAPS

I met Billy Collins, a rock star among poetry fans, after a benefit reading
he gave at the Herbst Theatre in San Francisco for California Poets in
the Schools. The date was January 15, 2004; I know because I kept the
sky-blue ticket stub to use as a souvenir bookmark. Backstage, a few of us
poet-teachers were mingling like groupies, talking with Billy—Billy!—who
told literary jokes and made us all laugh, one of us a little too loudly for
the situation. (It might have been me.) We wanted to ask him so many
questions about writing and simile-making and how it's humanly possible
to be so prolific, how he can be humorous and break hearts at the same
time. But Billy was on his way to another party, so he autographed our
books and bid us farewell. My friend Prartho and I thought about following him, but that would have been weird.

Recently I read that among the papers sold to the Ransom Center at
the University of Texas were some of Billy's jottings on scrap paper. This
caught my eye—Billy Collins without paper, writing on scraps? Really? I
thought *I* was the only one to write on Popsicle wrappers and scrounge the
depths of my shoulder bag for a stray receipt. But, no, Billy Collins told the
New York Times that while he was out walking around the city with no pen
and nothing to write on, the line of a poem occurred to him: "So I ducked
into a bank and started writing the poem on deposit slips," he told the
reporter. When a poem or idea—or an opening to a letter—is on its way
and about to move through you, you'd better write on whatever is handy.
No excuses. No waiting for the quiet and perfect desk setup and just-right
moleskin notebook. Rumor has it that J. K. Rowling concocted the name
Hogwarts on the back of an airplane sick bag, and I recently read in the
New Yorker that Bob Dylan penned a draft of "Like a Rolling Stone"
on stationery from the Roger Smith Hotel on 72nd Street. Somehow all
this writing on whatever is within reach or available reassured me. When
I have a grand idea and scribble with my blue eye pencil on the back of
a utility bill, I'm in fine company.

LETTER LEAD-IN

What might *you* write on in a pinch? Eucalyptus bark came to mind while I was hiking with Rasco this morning, so I picked up long stripes of bark and carried them back to the car. (Later I cut them into squares of stationery.) Purposely leave home without anything to write on or with and see what you find. By the way, a Sharpie on eucalyptus bark works surprisingly well.

Find a Story in the Dictionary

It's a marvel that all the words we use to talk, sing, tell stories, and write letters with can be found in one place: the dictionary. Of course, it's up to us to arrange random words into stanzas, sentences, and messages that mean something to ourselves and someone else. Locate a dictionary, the kind that's bound with a spine and has pages that flutter. Fish for favorite words. Gather a collection in the blank postcard space below. There's no limit. If you reel one in that's too small, toss it back. Or keep it for bait and see what else you can catch with it later.

My poet-pal Brian picks one large word from the dictionary to learn every day. He recently impressed me with his collection. We talked about how if you use a word three times, it's yours to keep. I told Brian that I like to be an amanuensis (secretary) to the day, alert to new words and phrases, taking dictation. Nodding, Brian immediately claimed *amanuensis* as his new word.

Arrange some of your most impressive words and connect them with others into the start of a story or poem. Mail this beginning to a well-chosen friend, like Brian.

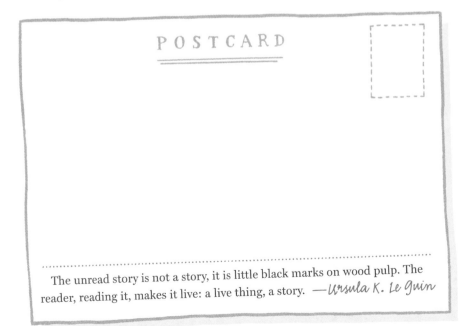

POSTCARD

The unread story is not a story, it is little black marks on wood pulp. The reader, reading it, makes it live: a live thing, a story. —*Ursula K. Le Guin*

The Invention of Paper

My son was doing some research on the invention of paper and shared his findings with me. I was surprised to learn that paper was invented in A.D. 105(!) and reported to the Chinese emperor by a man named Ts'ai Lun, an official of the imperial court. "The actual discovery was made by a eunuch named Cai Lun, a civil servant in Luoyang, China," Collin explained.

Cai used bark from mulberry trees and plant fiber, pounded it all into pulp, then dried and matted it into sheets. It was cheap and portable; light and strong and absorbent. A paper mold made from a four-sided bamboo frame was used to "dip up" the fiber slurry from the vat to hold it in place for drying. "Oh, I love the sound of 'fiber slurry,'" I called from the next room. I learned that eventually bamboo, tree bark, and other plant fibers were used in addition to hemp. Within a couple hundred years, paper took over from bamboo and silk to carry the written word. Advances were made. Thin strips of rounded bamboo stitched together with silk, flax, and animal hair was mixed into the molds. "Yellow dye was added for manuscript paper and doubled as an insect repellent," Collin said. "Pretty handy if you ask me," I said. (Mosquitoes love my son.) From China, papermaking moved to Korea. Then a Korean monk named Don-cho brought paper-making to Japan and shared his knowledge at the imperial palace.

"Wait, I'm lost," I said. "What's the time line?"

Collin sighed. "Pay attention, Mom. This happened sixty years *after* Buddhism was introduced in Japan." Chinese papermakers then spread their craft into Central Asia and Persia and eventually India, via traders.

"See?" I said to Collin on his iPad. "In an era of texts, tweets, likes, and links, paper still persists."

Collin looked up at me. "I know what you're going to say, Mom: 'May it never go away.'" (It was what I was going to say.)

You Supply the Middle

Find inspiration for a real or made-up story by picking up a book. Write down the opening and closing sentences—giving the author credit, of course—and then supply your own middle. For example, Dodie Smith's *I Capture the Castle* begins with, "I write this sitting in the kitchen sink," and ends with, "I love you. I love you. I love you." For the middle, I supplied: "I look out at the maple tree showing off her red and yellow leaves and think of the seasons we share." Or borrow a first sentence from one book and find an ending sentence from another book. Leave this mishmash of a one-sentence beginning connected to a one-sentence ending written with different colored pens as is, or be off and running to supply what happens next.

Ray Bradbury suggested the following technique for writers: "First find out what your hero wants, then just follow him." So what happens to *your* hero who's minding his own business, eating a ham and cheese sandwich at a local café? Look around back then for something to add to your story. Give something from your life to your hero.

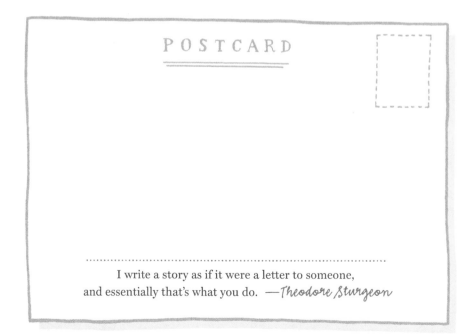

POSTCARD

I write a story as if it were a letter to someone,
and essentially that's what you do. —*Theodore Sturgeon*

Dear Reader,

The process of writing can be magical . . . mostly it's a process of putting one word after another. I try to change my superstitions with each project. Working in fountain pen is good because it slows me down just enough to keep my handwriting legible. Often I use two pens with different colored ink, so I can tell visually how much I did each day.

—Neil

A SAMPLE OF NEIL GAIMAN'S WRITING
From *Coraline*

> "Look—here's a piece of paper and a pen. Count all the doors and windows. List everything blue. Mount an expedition to discover the hot water tank. And leave me alone to work."
>
> "Can I go into the drawing room?"
>
> The drawing room was where the Joneses kept the expensive (and uncomfortable) furniture Coraline's grandmother had left when she died. Coraline wasn't allowed in there. Nobody went in there. It was only for best.
>
> "If you don't make a mess. And you don't touch anything."
>
> Coraline considered this carefully, then she took the paper and pen and went off to explore the inside of the flat.
>
> She discovered the hot water tank (it was in a cupboard in the kitchen).
>
> She counted everything blue (153).
>
> She counted the windows (21).
>
> She counted the doors (14).
>
> Of the doors that she found, thirteen open and closed.

The other—the big, carved, brown wooden door at the far corner of the drawing room—was locked. She said to her mother, "Where does that door go?"

"Nowhere, dear."

"It has to go somewhere."

NEIL GAIMAN writes books for readers of all ages and credits librarians with fostering his lifelong love of reading. He believes that he wouldn't be who he is without libraries. His happiest times as a boy were when he persuaded his parents to drop him off in the local library on their way to work. Born in the United Kingdom, he now lives in the United States.

100 Word Story

Lynn and Grant got together in cafés and each other's living rooms and hatched their plan for 100 Word Story. Writers of all stripes—memoir writers, fiction writers, essay writers, poets—from all over the world are invited to submit, in exactly one hundred words, their prose piece, story, slice of life memoir, or essay based on a photograph that Photo Editor Beret provides as the prompt.

Editor Lynn says, "Writers might think of the word count as the guard-rails put up around bowling lanes—it's a pleasing bit of structure and security." Editor Grant urges revision "as fervently as dentists recommend flossing." He also thinks the best hundred-word stories startle the reader and move with a sense of what's left out of the story. These stories are about absences and gaps, but they have a beginning, a middle, and an end. Lynn adds, "You would write one hundred words at a bus stop, on your lunch break, in your sleep. But with one hundred words, you must tell the whole story in its entirety, so it holds together like a perfect little dollhouse." Grant advises, "Always have something in the mail and keep hope alive. . . . It can strangely be more nurturing than actual success." Think of the space on the back of a postcard—they're that short. Submit your story at www.100wordstory.org.

Scarytales

By her own admission, Lynn was born too close to Halloween. Maybe that accounts for her wild imagination. I know firsthand that she carves the scariest faces on pumpkins, hands out the best candy on October 31, and has a razor-sharp sense of humor. She also wields a wicked pen and wrote a trilogy of one hundred–word stories titled *Scarytales*. She sent me "Red":

> *The girl always kept her face hidden by the deep, scarlet hood. She'd be gone days, loping down the woods' long-trod trails. Stories followed her like minnows after live bait—relentless, endless, ravenous. She'd jumped up and down on her grandmother's skeleton, howling. She could grow poison berries and bewitch you into eating them. She had a tail. Other children followed her to pet her warm back, then were never to be found. True, true, true, and true. But was her scent truly gamey, her smile really wolfish? Her innocence, like a dead leaf that lives off a green branch?*

Write a scary tale for a friend, and send it on a postcard for Halloween.

POSTCARD

Things are never quite as scary when you've got a best friend.
—*Bill Watterson*

The Day We Met

I met Lynn during my second year of college, in an Introduction to Theater Arts class. She told me later how she knew we'd be friends, remembering the black "goliath sandals" I was wearing that looked oh-so-cool. (Lynn loves shoes.) What I remember thinking was that the young woman who carried a neatly organized shoulder bag to class every Tuesday and pulled out a set of black pens that she arranged on her desk must take excellent notes. Our professor was visiting from England that year, so we recopied—and memorized—a lot of soliloquies. We might well have recited every line of Hamlet. It was a long to-be-or-not-to-be semester, but having Lynn as a new friend made everything more interesting.

The next summer, Lynn graduated and moved to Washington, D.C., for graduate school. That's when we started writing letters. We wrote through her emergency surgery, when a kidney stone dropped during her Faulkner final. ("I finished my final," she wrote. "What the hell was I thinking?") Through my graduation and move to San Francisco, getting a job at an art gallery, losing my father. Through her promotions, train trips to Connecticut to see her boyfriend, their small outdoor wedding. Through my early attempts at publication and getting into graduate school to meeting face-to-face again, when Lynn and her husband moved to San Francisco and rented an apartment around the corner from me.

Because of a young woman who knew how to share her life through stories and how to listen on and off the page, corresponding helped us build a lifelong, rock-solid friendship, something that makes being in the world feel adventurous and interesting, sane and kind.

LETTER LEAD-IN

Write a letter to a friend from school—elementary, junior high, high school, college, graduate school. Start by recounting your memory of the day you met.

Do You Remember?

Wendy Mass, the author of young adult and middle grade novels, gave me this idea. It's incredibly easy and could well be one of the most cherished gifts someone receives from you. All you have to do is find some special writing paper and a pen you like (my black calligraphy pen is what Collin reaches for when he writes a letter), then select one person you hold dear. You can, of course, pick more than one person, though I suggest writing to one at a time. Then simply recount a memory you have about the two of you, a time that's permanently inked in your heart. Begin with "Do you remember when we . . ." Write a few lines about something you shared. Ground it in small details. Tell her stuff she already knows. Fill one page of paper so she can frame it later, if she likes. Mail or hand-deliver it. This letter is a gift that's tied up with your hand, something real and solid, so a certain someone can bring a memory you made together back to life again.

POSTCARD

Writing is tied up with the hand, almost with a special nerve.
—Graham Greene

Dear Reader,

An e-mail from my grandmother would look just like an e-mail from anyone else. The typed words temporarily filling my screen would be whisked away in a few seconds as I opened the next e-mail in my inbox. Since it's incredibly rare to actually print out an e-mail, I will almost certainly never lay eyes on it again. But a handwritten letter from my grandmother, written on thin, lilac-scented paper in her delicate script, becomes a sacred object. I can hold it in my hands decades after she sent it to me, and remember how it lifted my sprits as a homesick ten-year-old away at camp for the first time. Holding that letter—and the literally hundreds of other letters and cards I've saved from family and friends over the years—instantly brings the writer, and that moment in time, rushing back to life. Tracing the raised letters that their pen made while it traveled across the pages, holding the same paper they held themselves, well, that's an irreplaceable experience.

I've started to frame special letters and I hang them on the wall like art. These include my four-year-old's proclamation in red marker that he loves me more than the universe (now I have proof to show him when he's a teenager!). And a letter my favorite author signed thanking me for a book I sent him. And a particularly funny note from my best friend in high school that she wrote during class and slipped into my pocket when we passed in the hall. Every time I walk by them, I'm reminded that a letter is a living, breathing thing and I'm grateful to have them. Write on!

Wendy

A SAMPLE OF WENDY MASS'S WRITING

From *Jeremy Fink and the Meaning of Life*

> "You can open it," I whisper, pushing the envelope across the seat to Lizzy.
>
> "No, you," she says, pushing it back.
>
> "You!" I toss it onto her lap, and she tosses it right back.
>
> "Oh, for goodness' sake," James says from the front seat. "I'll open it."
>
> Guiltily, I pass the envelope through the partially open window divider. I hear a ripping sound, which makes me cringe a little, and the letter appears a few seconds later. This one isn't as yellowed as the other one. I unfold it slowly.

WENDY MASS is the *New York Times* best-selling author of *The Candy-makers*, along with fifteen other novels for young readers, including *A Mango-Shaped Space*, *Jeremy Fink and the Meaning of Life*, and *Every Soul a Star*. She is currently writing the sequel to *The Candymakers* while building a labyrinth in her backyard in New Jersey. Not at the same time, of course. That'd be weird. Visit her at http://wendymass.com.

The Line of a Letter

My dear friend Prartho was born in Maine, then moved to New York and back and forth to India a few times, before landing in California. She has been writing poems and letters for most of her life and is a sought-after Poet in the Schools. Three years ago, she was awarded a fellowship to get her MFA at Syracuse University, so she packed her bags and books once again, said good-bye to her first- and second-grade student-mystics and all her poet-pals, and settled in for three long winters on the East Coast to write and teach and shovel her walkway piled high with snow.

Now, back in California, she recently won a book award from Lynx House Press, which will publish her full-length collection, *Elephant Raga*. (*Raga* means "color" or "passion" in the classical music of India.) I am so happy for her. I'm also inspired that she held on to her artistic sensibilities and, between traveling the world and receiving critiques from fellow students, never gave up on her big dream. But how can she know any of this if I don't tell her? So I put pen to paper, make a few curves, twists, turns, and loop-de-loop patterns, and let my words meander:

Hey, P., dog at my feet, boy at school, the morning racing in all directions as my thoughts drift to you, your good news, a late summer gust carrying heartfelt congratulations to your mailbox . . . Your satchel of poems has found a home! With much joy, K.

LETTER LEAD-IN

Stay put and send your heart out to someone via a meandering line of time. Share something that they've done that gave you a happy high. Add curlicues to the address, dash a few sparks on the envelope. (I sketched an elephant, trunk facing up for good luck.) Include a small doodle along the seal to hint of what's to come.

SENDING SILLY PRESENTS EVERY SO OFTEN

During our thirty-year friendship, Lynn and I have gone through a few dry spells when we've let too much time slip by between letters and phone calls and visits, even though we live only forty-five minutes away from each other. Once, after too many sunrises and sunsets, I sent her a small vial of Amma Rose perfume, blessed by the hugging saint herself. Another time, after I had knee surgery and had to remain on the couch for a few months, it was Lynn who wrote me a letter every few days, to cheer me up. In one, she included a notepad—with a mountain goat stamped on the front—and asked when I could hoof it up the fifty-six steps to my car and drive across the bridge to meet at our favorite Iraqi restaurant, Zatar. Send someone you haven't reached out to in a while, and whose friendship you don't want to dry out, a silly little present. If you need ideas, read on.

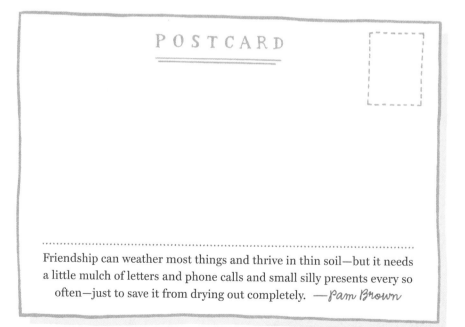

POSTCARD

Friendship can weather most things and thrive in thin soil—but it needs a little mulch of letters and phone calls and small silly presents every so often—just to save it from drying out completely. —*Pam Brown*

Gifts to Include in an Envelope

You don't have to spend a cent on a gift. Simply tuck a little something extra in a dashed-out note or letter. Bryce sent me my horoscope yesterday taped to a homemade postcard made from a donut box and wished me success. This made my entire day.

A small notepad with a silly image on the front
Good advice
A wishing stone
A crossword puzzle
A maple leaf or sprig of lavender
A balloon and a piece of string
A comic strip
A horoscope
A photograph of you and a friend
A feather
The fortune from a fortune cookie
A piece of taffy
A stick of gum
A bookmark
A favorite recipe
A handwritten poem
A handful of beads and string
An origami swan or turtle
A shell (sand optional)
A dandelion, aka wishweed
A pair of socks
An encouraging word
A favorite pen

BUTTER TOFFEE PEANUTS

Kristin and Gina and I were friends from elementary school. We lived in the same neighborhood and all attended YMCA camp together each summer. Because Y-Camp participants are encouraged to help pay for part of their camp experience, a few months before we left for Boulder Creek on that yellow bus, we had to sell several cartons each of sugar-toasted butter toffee peanuts, with the Y-Camp logo printed on every can.

We'd already proven that it was impossible to eat just one peanut—we *had* to sample a few—so we hatched our plan. After school and on weekends, we'd carry our cartons down to the shopping center on McKee Avenue and claim our territory between Clifford's Drugstore and the Bank of America. Since we already knew that no one could resist a sample, we cracked open a can and offered freebies to people going into the bank, politely suggesting that they take out an extra $10, "Help a kid earn her way to camp. Buy a can or two of butter toffee peanuts." This became our motto. It's what we wrote on our signs. At ten years old, we were savvy marketers.

We sold hundreds of cans of butter toffee peanuts this way. Each week-end, we'd walk home with empty boxes and wads of cash in our pockets. On our way, we'd talk about Camp Campbell, where we'd sing our voices hoarse, swim and hike, row boats and shoot arrows, and make more lanyards than any child really needs to make in one lifetime. And, of course, during nap time we'd write letters home from our bunks, telling our parents how we were and that we never wanted to eat another butter toffee peanut again. Until next summer, of course.

LETTER LEAD-IN

Celebrate a summer activity. Send a friend a lanyard or a recipe or a candy bar you used to like. I received a case of YMCA butter toffee peanuts one year as a birthday gift from Kristin. A rush of memories followed after I signed for my package and pried the silver flip-top off the first can.

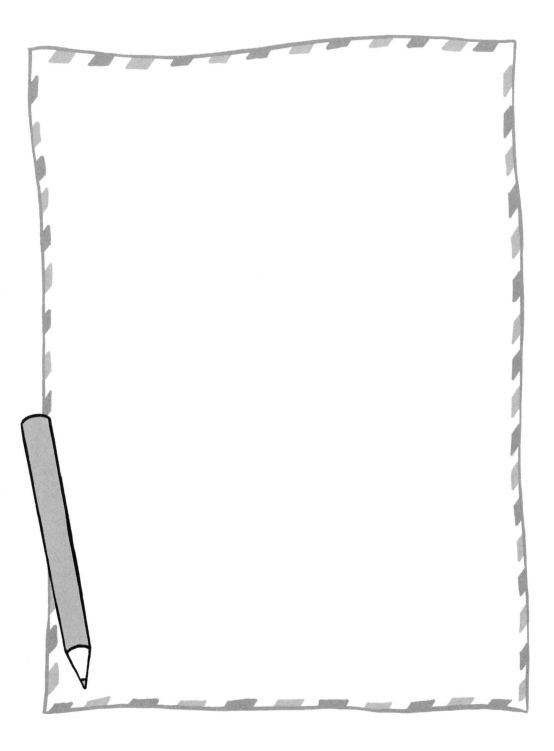

REMINDERS, SUGGESTIONS, GOOD LUCK, ADVICE

Start a postcard or letter with a friendly reminder, such as "Hey, check out the full moon on the twelfth," or "Let's meet and watch for shooting stars." Or begin with some good advice: "Never write a letter while you're angry," or "Don't do laps in a pool during a lightning storm."

You can make your entire letter an offering of good luck with small drawings or include the real thing—a four-leaf clover (the three-leaf variety will do in a pinch; the odds of finding a four-leaf clover are 10,000 to 1), a wishbone, an acorn, or a paper garland of elephants with upturned trunks, since elephants are a symbol of friendship. Or suggest some good luck–generating activities, like catching ladybugs and setting them free or listening to crickets (their sound symbolizes wisdom and prosperity). Dragonflies, a sprig of bamboo, a stray eyelash (who knew?), charms in the shape of a hand, a key, a crescent, a ladder: all are said to bring good luck. Oh, and don't forget the power of the heads-up or tails-never-fails lucky penny.

POSTCARD

Learn to recognize good luck when it's waving at you, hoping to get your attention. —*Sally Koslow*

Dear Reader,

To write a letter is one thing. To write a poem is another. To write a letter as a poem in your own glorious hand is an entirely different escapade altogether—a grand journey into sound into body into love. Such a rare thing these fragile twenty-first-century days: to handwrite a letter, a poem. Key word is *hand*, as in handed forth, offered from the body, complete with the energy of the body sizzling from the stalactite-riddled depths of your heart, blasting up to your head like a bolt of *what*? *Lightning*? No, a bolt of gold-threaded bodily genius, now ziggurat-fox trotting around in your skull for a time, before shooting down your arm, wresting past your wrists, through your pianist-nervy fingers, rattling the pen like a glassy wand and . . . *surprise*! What a journey! You're invited in.

Write on,

Albert

A SAMPLE OF ALBERT FLYNN DeSILVER'S WRITING

From *Letters to Early Street*

EXCERPT FROM LETTER FIFTY

Dear Marian,

Today I fill an envelope with a fragile, limited edition,
endangered ecosystem. It fits nicely in a #10 I send
to you in midtown Manhattan. I immediately feel
prompt, courteous, and dependable. The postman disagrees,
says writing "FRAGILE" on the envelope is crying wolf,
so I bite him in the leg . . . A pile of rose petals on the paisley
table is my desk. Such a despondent wolf I am, scuttling off

with a mess of bills, letters, & postal pant legs in my mouth.
You called to say your cat ate one of the written upon illegible petals
I sent you in that #10. Which one was it?
Histrionic, anticipatorily, yours—
Any or all of the above?

Love, Al

(*Burp!* ... *meow*, says the cat.)

ALBERT FLYNN DESILVER is an internationally published poet, author, and speaker. His poetry collections include *Letters to Early Street* (all originally handwritten) and the memoir *Beamish Boy*. He hosts literary events, teaches writing and mindfulness workshops, and is finishing his first novel. Visit the virtual version of him at www.albertflynndesilver.com.

SEND A GROUCH A COMPLIMENT

In my neighborhood, there's a man who I've never seen smile and who frequently yells at his dog. After attending a benefit for the Tibetan Society at which His Holiness the Dalai Lama spoke about kindness, I arrived home and decided to make a mental adjustment to have kind thoughts toward others be the focus of my practice: "to expand my heart out to others, to not think badly about others." This is what the Dalai Lama encourages, reminding us that we have a precious human life and should not waste it. He has written numerous letters to the Chinese government in an attempt to open a peaceful dialogue; I could at least reach out to this man who takes up *two* parking spaces in front of my house and yells at his dog. I'll be honest, it's challenging. I have to keep looking for things about him that might allow my heart to soften. Yesterday, when I was taking out the recycling, I heard him say to his four-legged furry friend, "Please get in the damn car, Coco!" It's a start.

Pen a compliment for someone who could probably really use it. The grouchiest person in your neighborhood, say, or an elderly person who may not get out much. Leave it under their porch mat or on their car.

POSTCARD

Be kind whenever possible. It is always possible.
—*His Holiness the Fourteenth Dalai Lama*

Three Hundred Sixty-Five Thank-Yous

John Kralik is a man who knows firsthand that writing a thank-you letter a day can become an act of gratitude that can change your entire life. John was in a major slump—overweight, getting divorced, fighting to keep his business afloat, estranged from his children, living in an apartment he didn't like. And if this weren't already a laundry list from hell, his girlfriend had just broken up with him. His life changed radically, though, when he decided to stop focusing on what he didn't have and find some way to be grateful for what he *did* have.

On a New Year's Day hike, he turned things around by committing to actively—the key word being *actively*—look for something specific to be grateful for every single day. Some large or small kindness he felt blessed by and could express appreciation for. The writing of a simple thank-you note became his daily practice for a whole year, after he'd (ironically) received a card from the girlfriend who had broken up with him, thanking him for a Christmas gift he'd given her.

John got organized. He began to handwrite his thank-you notes to loved ones, coworkers, friends, business associates, store clerks, doctors, neighbors, strangers, even the barista who made his coffee and remembered his name. John's fate was sealed. And guess what happened? His whole life reoriented itself. John stepped through the gateway of gratitude right into the hall of happiness. He lost weight, found inner peace, gained true friendship, and is now a superior court judge in Los Angeles and the author of the memoir *356 Thank Yous*.

LETTER LEAD-IN

Write a letter of thanks to someone in your life. Write one letter a week to seven people. Write one letter a month to thirty people. Match or break John's 365-letters-a-year record.

KINDS OF CORRESPONDENCE

Which kind of correspondence haven't you signed, sealed, and sent in a while or longer? Ever? Make a point—aka *commit*—to write one from this list in the next week. If the letter you want to write isn't on this list—add it. Then write it.

A thank-you note
A get well letter
A love letter
A sympathy card
A note of apology
A congratulations card
A fan letter
A letter of request
A letter of protest
A form letter
A letter to the editor
A friendly "just because" letter
A good advice letter
A postcard
An invitation
A pen pal letter
A letter written with invisible ink
A "let's change the world together" letter
A letter that names all your favorite places to eat
A "turn this into a song" letter
A "good things are happening and you're who I want to tell" letter
An "I'm sorry your dog is sick, I love him too" letter
A "here's a funny story that really happened" letter
A letter that lists what you're grateful for

Get Thee to a Snail Mail
Revival Shop Posthaste!

James Tucker and Risa Culbertson opened a shop called The Aesthetic Union for those of us who prefer paper and ink and the handwritten and hand-printed word. They have two manual presses, one circa 1910 and the other from 1984. If you can't imagine what a manual press looks like, conjure up an oversized piece of black inky machinery, with lots of moving parts that makes a *thwappa-thwappa-thwappa* sound. Does that help? James and Risa use their manual presses to create greeting cards and posters and all kinds of cool art prints.

Collin and I wandered inside yesterday en route to Dynamo Doughnuts and ended up staying for Letter Writing Tuesday. James and Risa provided us with paper, envelopes, pens—even stamps. We sat at old-fashioned wooden desks to write and write. Collin wrote to his dad. I wrote to Collin. There are stools around a large wooden table where others sat to write and write. There's even a manual typewriter set up near the front door to type and type. James and Risa sell airmail envelopes, leather journals, Japanese paper tape (I bought a roll of pink tape with red polka dots), dead-stock stationery, Blackwing pencils, and cards that are "cheeky," as Collin's British grandma is fond of saying. Collin even found a birthday card for his grandpa. Across the front in splashy orange lettering it reads, "You're a big ol' jar of awesome sauce."

SOME POSTAGE REQUIRED

The Aesthetic Union
555 Alabama Street
San Francisco, CA 94110

Between Brain, Hands, and Pen

Japanese and Chinese calligraphers believe there's a mysterious connection between the brain, the hands, and the pen—that there's this *flow* that's created between them, bringing about a strange yet strong power. I believe this too. So does my friend, the calligrapher and poet Sandy Diamond. I have one of Sandy's framed cards by my front door, reminding me in uppercase black lettering with a swirl of gray and crimson that "Artists Are Healed By Their Art." It's signed in Sandy's gossamer-penciled hand, her first and last names all lowercase and run together. Sandy writes on the backs of maps and recycled slips of paper from old manuscript pages. She'd slide notes under my door when we were neighbors one winter in Langley, Washington. In her tiny, thin-tipped printing that resembles blackbirds circling the sky of the page, she wrote, "hello, comrade in calligraphy, fa fa fa friend forever. wishing you writing bliss." Pick up a calligraphy pen and concentrate for a while with that mysterious connection created between your brain, hands, and pen. Write something of truth or memory to a friend in your unique hand and slide it under her door.

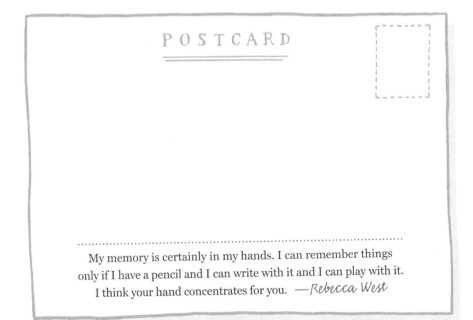

POSTCARD

My memory is certainly in my hands. I can remember things only if I have a pencil and I can write with it and I can play with it. I think your hand concentrates for you. —*Rebecca West*

Dear Reader,

A teacher of mine, Kazuaki Tanahashi, taught me this: when we draw, we leave ourselves behind in the lines that we make. We leave evidence of our wishes for our children, and for their children. He was talking about drawing, but writing shows us ourselves in the same way. The white page is perfect. It is like silence in music. Silence is perfect. What are you going to add? What are you going to bring? What can you bring? What you can bring is yourself, your heart, your goodness, your hope. Our senses are what we use to find out about the world. When we touch a piece of paper, and we hold a pencil or a pen or a brush, we have the most direct line from our heart to its expression.

—Jon

A SAMPLE OF JON J MUTH'S WRITING
From *Zen Shorts*

The next day, Addy went to have tea with Stillwater.

"Hello?" Addy said as she stepped inside.

"Come in! Come in!" a faraway voice called.

Then she heard the voice say, "Oh, yes . . . Come out! Come out!" Stillwater was in the backyard. He was in a tent.

"This is a birthday present from my Uncle Ry," Stillwater said.

"He always gives presents on his birthday, to celebrate the day he was born. I like it so much, that I'm not staying in my house right now."

Stillwater invited Addy to sit with him.

"You brought me some cake!" said Stillwater. "That was very nice of you. Is it your birthday?" he asked.

"No," said Addy.

"It's not mine, either," said Stillwater. "But let me give you a gift for my uncle's birthday. I will tell you a story."

JON J MUTH'S highly acclaimed picture books are beloved around the world and have been translated into more than ten languages. He lives in upstate New York with his wife and four children, where he spends time "chasing the clouds from his brushes."

Something to Write With

The importance of a new pen cannot be emphasized enough as a source for letter-writing inspiration. Today, Rasco Roon and I took a field trip to find just the right pen. We arrived at Mill Valley Services, where Eric greeted us and Trisha waved from her desk. Rasco sniffed one of the copiers, then sat on the carpet, knowing this could take awhile. I tested fine-tips, rolling writers, extra-thick calligraphy pens. I tried out every color—jet black, royal blue, postal red. I wrote on the small, white notepad that Jan, the owner, sets out for people like you and me who have to try our pens before we buy them. I couldn't decide, so I bought the five I liked best. On our walk home, my bag of new pens in one hand and Rasco's leash in the other, he led the way while I considered other writing possibilities. I stepped over a hopscotch outline and thought of chalk, spotted a grill and imagined a chunk of charcoal. At home, I looked at the container of crayons I keep for when I'm in a coloring kind of mood. I sat with magic cat Clive in the garden, ate an almond butter sandwich, and considered dipping pine needles into a pot of ink. I remembered reading how the artist Paul Klee, after finishing a bowl of chocolate pudding, scraped the tines of his fork along the bottom to make a design. Clive stretched out on the warm pebbles near the Ping-Pong table and I thought of our friend Mike, who stopped by to say hi last week and, finding no one home and without a pen, left a note written in pebbles on the Ping-Pong table: "No pen. Miss you guys! Mike." In true Mike fashion, a heart enclosed his message.

LETTER LEAD-IN

Test a few pens to find the one you like best. In the blank space on the next page, write the names of people to whom you'd like to send a short note but haven't gotten around to yet. Or leave someone a simple note using unconventional material. Or buy two identical pens and mail one with a letter to a pen-loving friend!

Types of Pens

Besides having friends to talk with and confide in, pens are the best. Miguel de Cervantes once said, "The pen is the tongue of the mind." Pens don't have to be recharged or plugged in. They don't cost much. They're easy to carry, and you'll probably never have to remove one from your pocket, backpack, or shoulder bag and put it in a gray plastic tray at airport security. At least, I've never been asked to remove *my* pen, though I've had to remove pretty much everything else. There's a pen out there that's perfect for every hand; every situation; every note, card, letter, invitation, and RSVP.

ballpoint
rollerball
Pentel Slicci pens—for fine, smooth lines

crayon
felt tip fineliner
Pilot V pens—for a strong line
quill

uni-ball Jetstream permanent rollerball pen—the pen of the people

Kuretake Zig Cartoonist Mangaka Outline Pen—the go-to plastic-tip pen

MUJI pens—for great flow, whether writing or sketching
pencil

calligraphy
Mont Blanc pens—the most expensive at $450(!)

Zebra Sarasa Clip—for supersharp lines
Sharpie
fountain pen

The Seven Year Pen—enough ink to write 1.7 meters a day for seven years

P.S. Apparently only one type of ink—the kind in gel pens—is counterfeit-proof to acetone or any other chemical used in "check washing." An expert who consults for law enforcement and corporations on "the art of the steal" says he personally signs all his checks and important documents with the uni-ball Gel Impact pen ($2). He's a pretty careful guy and only allowed me to print this if I didn't reveal his name!

HOMEMADE INVISIBLE INK

Mix 1 spoon baking powder with 1 to 2 spoons of cold water. Dip a cotton swab in the mixture and use it to write your message on a piece of white paper. After the ink dries, hold the paper up to a lightbulb and your message will appear. You can also "paint the paper" with purple grape juice to reveal your secret message.

HANDWRITING IN THE AIR

My friend Claire is a wildly inventive poet and teacher who is an expert at helping kids believe in themselves. She is a Poet in the Schools, a tutor, and an adviser for the Poetry Out Loud program. It's the kids who are referred to as "pull-outs" that Claire often works with. It's the parents of these kids who ask her to guide them in exactly how to help their children succeed with writing. Six feet tall with sparkling blue eyes and a ready smile, Claire has been known to show up in classrooms dressed as Bird Woman, complete with a headdress of feathers. She has no fear and keeps many tricks up her sleeves when it comes to experimenting with inspiring a child to play with words on a blank page. When one of her students has a hard time gripping a pen or pencil and making those up-and-down curvy strokes that form letters, Claire whips out her paper with railroad dashed lines, and they play little drill-like games.

Claire and I talked on the phone this morning, bemoaning how handwriting is no longer taught after second grade. "Don't get me started," she said. Claire told me about how she had a group of students stand behind her recently and mimic the linear lines of movement she made with her hand—the downward stroke, the coming into a loop at the bottom, the traveling up into a little curl at the top. She confided that she knows how these kids feel: "Growing up, I moved from New Jersey to California during second grade and somehow missed the Q-R-S part of the alphabet," she laughed. "At least I got the beginning and the end, though." Claire understands what these kids are going through, looking at the world and wanting to write, to share a story, but being a little bit stuck with how to do this through words on a page. So she shows her students the slanted ovals in the air before they go to a tabletop to practice moving their hands over a large hard surface. Finally, they move on to the rectangle of paper, where their loosened-up arms, hands, and fingers can make cursive letters in ink. What they see reflected in Claire's eyes is the belief that they, too, can write poems and stories and share them with her, their parents, their teachers, the rest of the class, their friends. We all see and write the world differently, and we don't want anyone to be left out.

LETTER LEAD-IN

Different parts of a letter or note are like a ceremony that you tweak, look over, wrap up by sealing, and then send on its way. Do a handwriting dance in the air, then write something in cursive to a special friend (recopy a recipe or a poem), to someone who's wild and imaginative like Claire. Or maybe write it on a kite and fly it high in the air.

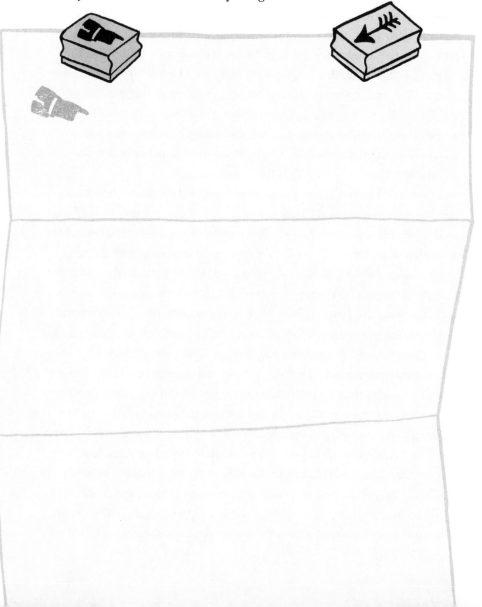

Change Your Handwriting

We have to play with what we want to get good at. Shooting baskets to make that three-point swish during a high-pressure game, baking multiple lemon soufflés, even remembering to write postcards to our friends—and to ourselves—when we go on vacation. Signing our name, like practicing our penmanship, takes practice. Write your own name—and nicknames—in as many styles as you can. Keep your wrist relaxed, allowing your hand to move so the letters flow and the forming of your name can be a whole-body physical experience. Let your hands dance and twirl across the page, signing your autograph with a few sensational scribbles thrown in. Make art out of the letters of your name: large scrawls, sideways slants, uppercase loops. Include the smudges and cross-outs too. Find a look you're happy with and take this new looser signature style for a test-write. Continue to practice by making a list of your favorite things or by telling someone what you adore about them: "I love how you rescue spiders from sinks," "how you slice a ripe peach and share it with me," "how when you ride your bike you smell like the wind." Things like that.

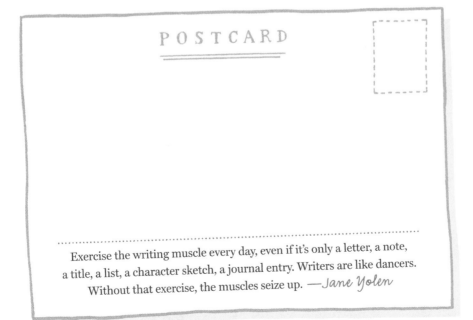

POSTCARD

Exercise the writing muscle every day, even if it's only a letter, a note, a title, a list, a character sketch, a journal entry. Writers are like dancers. Without that exercise, the muscles seize up. —*Jane Yolen*

Eight Facts about Writing by Hand

Fact #1: Something happens between brain and hand and eye. Maybe that's why 70 percent of writers across all genres do first drafts on legal pads.

Fact #2: Handwriting is no longer being taught in school past the second grade. (Sigh.) Massachusetts is one of several states, however, that wants to keep penmanship lessons in the curriculum.

Fact #3: Paper isn't plugged in to the distraction-filled Internet. Obvious, yes, but worth noting again (and again).

Fact #4: The motion of your hand as you write calms the nervous system and forges important creative connections, engages your motor skills, and keeps your mind sharp.

Fact #5: Areas of your brain light up when you write words by hand versus just studying the words closely.

Fact #6: Elementary school students who write essays with a pen not only write *more* than their keyboard-tapping friends, but they write faster and in more complete sentences too. So there.

Fact #7: When you form the shapes that create letters, your hand is working harder and creating more neural connections than when you select a button with a character on it.

Fact #8: Knowing someone's handwriting can be a marker of a friendship's longevity.

Another Way to Respond to a Text

Cristina Vanko decided she was tired of texting. She needed some major digital detox. But she still wanted to keep in touch with all her texting friends. What could she do? One morning Cristina woke up and knew. She gave herself an assignment. Her version of keeping in touch with her texting friends would look like this: she would answer their texts, *but* she would only do so by hand, writing her messages out in calligraphy and texting a photograph of her note. Her father—like mine—had loved calligraphy, and she now had his pen. She was all set. She pushed aside the keyboard. She would *not* touch it. She would spell out every word by hand.

Every time she got a text, she'd "promptly" respond by putting her father's pen to paper and snapping a photo of what she'd just written; then and only then would she send her response via text. It took awhile. Some of her friends didn't understand why they weren't hearing back from her right away like they usually did. Some friends got annoyed and impatient. Cristina did this for an entire week. Yes, it can be done. Yes, it took a lot longer than tapping out her reply in abbreviations. But her friends were genuinely touched. "OMG, Cristina, Really?" "Seeing your writing made me feel *soooo* close to you, like you are really here with me." Some friends shared the notes she wrote on the Internet. Cristina was asked to give a TEDx talk about her experiment in answering texts via handwriting. She even got a book deal. "Technology is easy. Real relationships take time," she says. After the week, she realized the assignment she'd given herself was a way for her personality to shine through via her handwriting.

LETTER LEAD-IN

For one day—even one hour!—give yourself Cristina's assignment. Your pen need not be a calligraphy pen. I bet your friends will thank you, too.

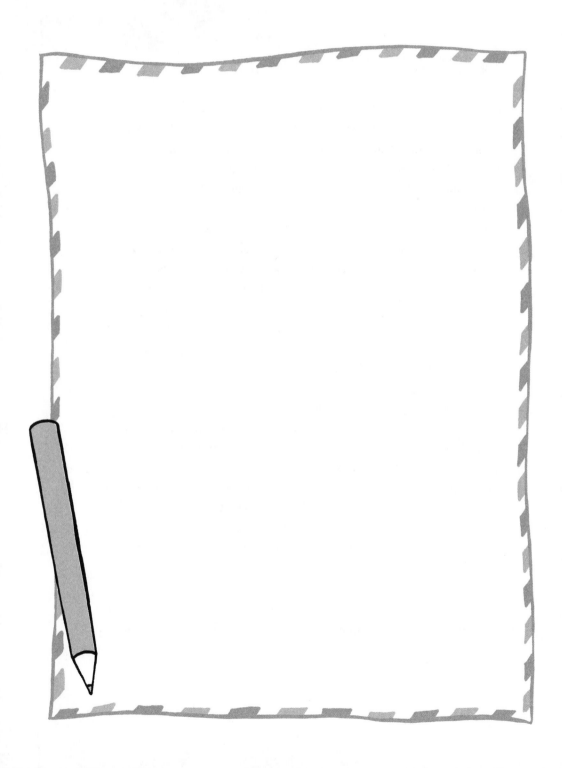

Dear Reader,

A Confession: I like my own handwriting. It isn't beautiful, or orderly. The j's and g's and y's are hard to tell apart, t's go uncrossed and i's undotted, and the whole thing slants alarmingly across the white page like a drunken polar bear's tracks across the tundra. But that's what I like about it, its imperfections, even its illegibility. It's *mine*, like my unruly hair, my crooked nose, my fingerprints. Sometimes when I'm sitting in my car writing, I feel like I'm following these looping black tracks rather than creating them—they're guiding me someplace I don't know how to reach any other way.

Love,

Alison

A SAMPLE OF ALISON LUTERMAN'S WRITING

From *The Secret of My Success*

I am writing this in the parking lot of Walgreens, where I just purchased a couple of manuscript mailers, a new brand of anti-frizz serum for my hair (hope springs eternal!), a discounted day-after-Easter bunny (solid milk chocolate, fifty cents), and a small tablet of light purple eye shadow. Now, this is the life: I can apply the eye shadow in the rear-view mirror and check how it looks (too light), eat my chocolate bunny without sharing, and write.

Every once in a while, people who come to my writing workshops ask me how I'm so productive. Because I've been published, they think that I must have superior work habits. Nothing could be further from the truth. The people who ask about my productivity are inevitably parents who work full time and can't seem to squeeze in the requisite twenty minutes of writing a day between board meetings and Little League. They blame themselves. They imagine that if only they could get up a half-hour earlier in the mornings, or manage their time better, they too could be published and happy.

I'm sure that somewhere out there is a writer with such superb work habits, but I am not that person. I am lazy and teach part-part-part time and spend the rest of my day reading clothing catalogs and complaining on the phone to my girlfriends. If I did have children, I would probably forget to feed them.

For me, the answer to the question "When do you write?" is easy: I write when I'm avoiding some other important task. For example, this essay is being written on April 23, and my taxes are not yet done. I also write when the bathroom needs cleaning, when the garden needs weeding, or when I'm skipping an important meeting. Paperwork is always good for a poem. When my California Poets in the Schools contracts are due, my muse gets particularly busy.

ALISON LUTERMAN has written three books of poetry: *The Largest Possible Life*, *See How We Almost Fly*, and *Desire Zoo*. Her essays have appeared in *Salon*, *The Sun Magazine*, *The L.A. Review*, *The New York Times' Modern Love*, and elsewhere. She lives in an old neighborhood in Oakland, California, with her husband, two cats, a fig tree, two peach trees, a lemon tree, and a guava tree that drops its fruit all over the driveway.

Another Name to Write With

I was named for my mother's younger sister, who had a winning sense of humor. I was also named after my father's sister, Ann, who loved to play the guitar and ride horses. Karen means "pure"; Ann, "gracious"; and Benke, "blessed." Lucky me! For my nom de plume or literary double, I use the nickname my mother gave me, Katrina ("popularity"), and my son's middle name, Trelawny. (Edward John Trelawny was an English adventurer, a novelist, and a close friend of the poet Percy Bysshe Shelley.) Writer Joyce Carol Oates suggests to her students that they write under a pseudonym for a week, since writing under a different name can allow for a lot of freedom. Freedom they may not ordinarily have when they identify with the names they've worn all their lives.

What pseudonym—pen or secret writing name—would you choose for yourself? Take your time. Do some research. Be adventuresome when selecting. Choose from the heart. Write to a friend using the name you've chosen for yourself and give the backstory of why you chose it. Maybe suggest a pseudonym for your friend.

POSTCARD

Names have power. —*Rick Riordan, The Lightning Thief*

Pseudonyms and Pen Names of Famous Writers

Some authors choose what's called a pen name to disguise their gender. Joanne Rowling shortened her name to a set of initials—she borrowed the K from her grandmother Kathleen. Some authors choose to make their name more distinctive or avoid the spotlight and write under a secret name, or pseudonym. When J. K. Rowling decided to write novels for adults, she chose the secret name Robert Galbraith, in part to avoid the public's expectations and also to hear what critics had to say when they didn't know the book they were reviewing was by the amazing author of the Harry Potter series. Who can blame her?

Karen Blixen wrote under the name Isak Dinesen.

Howard Allen Frances O'Brien writes under Anne Rice.

Theodor Seuss Geisel used the name Dr. Seuss.

Joe Klein, while writing *Primary Colors*, simply wrote under Anonymous.

Alisa Zinov'yevna Rosenbaum wrote under Ayn Rand.

Agatha Christie also wrote under the name Mary Westmacott.

Benjamin Franklin wrote under a few names, including Silence Dogood and Anthony Afterwit.

Clive Staples Lewis wrote under C. S. Lewis and N. W. Clerk.

Samuel Clemens wrote under Mark Twain.

Stephen King wrote some novels under the name Richard Bachman.

A Secret Admirer

Collin and Ryan share a love of tennis and basketball, creek walking and
stone skipping, Ping-Pong and sleepovers . . . and writing. Both thirteen
years old, they don't have any classes together this semester but do
volunteer on the same Friday at a senior center called The Redwoods.
They work with Fred in the garden shoveling compost into a wheelbarrow
(yuck!) and sometimes help out in the flower-arranging class. They escort
residents to poetry readings and music events in the multipurpose room.
Collin's been known to check a few hearing aids; Ryan likes serving tea
and coffee in the dining hall. On Valentine's Day, they dig through my basket
of student poems, select a stack of favorites, and write individual notes
on the backs that read, "You're loved and thought of today. —A Secret
Admirer." They deliver the poems to the residents' mailboxes next to the
front office in the lobby, hoping no one sees them. Afterward, they walk
around handing out chocolates. One man asks, "How much, son?" When
they run out of chocolates, they open the backup bag of butterscotch
candies, until the lady at the check-in desk says, "Please, boys, don't. The
residents can choke." When they pile into the backseat of my car, I ask
what they did with the rest of the candy. "We had to eat it," Ryan explains.
To which Collin adds, "We didn't have a choice."

LETTER LEAD-IN

Find a senior center in your town. It doesn't matter how old or young
you are, sending someone a poem or note with "You're loved" or "Someone thinks you're special" and signing it "A Secret Admirer" will be well
received. Tip: include soft-center chocolates, *not* hard candy. Or maybe
tangerines. Your choice.

ELAINE'S ENVELOPES

Elaine makes homemade envelopes. She uses newspapers, grocery bags, sheet music, old maps, and gift wrap. Sometimes Elaine sends letters with just one word written inside: "Hello!" But those one-word notes sealed in her exquisite envelopes are exceptional treasures to receive. She also likes stamps. "Do you want to see the new Year of the Horse stamp?" she asked when our paths crossed at the farmer's market last Tuesday. "They just came out. I bought three sheets." My answer was "of course," so we walked back to her car where she reached into the passenger side and pulled out her golden Year of the Horse stamps, all pink edges and shiny manes. "They won't last long," she cautioned. "Go now." Well, you can see how seriously Elaine takes her stamps. I admire that.

Follow Elaine's example and make your own envelope from some found piece of paper that you fold just so (or open an already-made envelope and use it as a template). Write one word inside, seal it with some tape, and you'll be all set to send it to a stamp-loving friend.

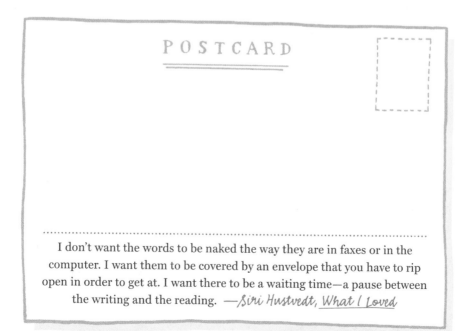

POSTCARD

I don't want the words to be naked the way they are in faxes or in the computer. I want them to be covered by an envelope that you have to rip open in order to get at. I want there to be a waiting time—a pause between the writing and the reading. —*Siri Hustvedt, What I Loved*

A Friendship That Started with a Housefly

Illustrator Edward Gorey and writer Peter F. Neumeyer met on a sailing trip in Cape Cod. It was a day-trip their editor had arranged. Out on the water, the two didn't have much to say. When they got back to the dock, Edward—aka Ted—put one foot on the pier when, all of a sudden, the dinghy scooted out from under him and he fell between. Peter, with quick reflexes, grabbed Ted's arm to help him up but accidentally dislocated Ted's shoulder in the process (ouch). The two men finally started talking in the hospital waiting room, since they had to wait for several hours to see a doctor. It was here they struck up a long conversation about writing and illustrating and stories.

That meeting of creative minds also involved a watercolor of a housefly that Edward had drawn, and a friendship followed during a thirteen-month period when they collaborated on three children's books. Peter wrote the text, and Edward drew the illustrations. Letters and postcards flew back and forth between them. Luckily Peter kept all the envelopes that Edward had whimsically addressed to him. Edward Gorey was a man who cared deeply about the welfare of all living creatures—cats, dogs, whales, birds, bats, insects, invertebrates. This love was reflected in the drawings (yeah, okay, sometimes a little creepy) he made on specially illustrated envelopes for the notes and letters he sent to Peter. On one, a blue lizard with a banner in his mouth is holding Peter's address. On another, a white bat is flying toward the moon with Peter's name in his claws. In yet another, a reptilian creature is hanging from a blanket hooked to a zip line above Peter's street address, city, state, and zip code. Who wouldn't want to receive a letter in an envelope like *that*?

Floating Worlds is a collection of Peter and Edward's letters and pictures of Edward's envelopes. My cat, Clive, loves Edward Gorey's illustrations too. Turns out, Gorey illustrated T. S. Eliot's *Old Possum's Book of Practical Cats*.

LETTER LEAD-IN

Find a picture you like—either one you've drawn or one you've cut out of a magazine—and glue or tape it to the front of an envelope, leaving space to write a friend's name and address around, above, across, inside, or to the left or right of it. Perhaps you'll include some special message along the envelope's seal. Or include SWAK (sealed with a kiss) if you feel that way.

My editor, who actually takes time to send handwritten notes—yes, I know, I'm pretty lucky—was in line at a post office in Boston and was shocked to see that a college-aged man in front of her needed the postal clerk to explain how to address an envelope. You know, on what line to put the recipient's first and last name, street address, city, state, and zip code. And where the return—sender's—address should go. We've gotten so used to e-mailing letters that perhaps a little refresher is needed.

The return address is where you, the sender, write your name, street address, city, state, and zip code on the front of the envelope or package, in the upper left-hand corner. "Why bother with a return address?" you might ask. Well, let's say someone wants to write back to you. Or let's say the person you're writing to has moved and there's no forwarding address, and the post office needs to return your letter. There are other reasons, but these are the most common.

In the center of the envelope is where you put the name, street address, city, state, and zip code of the person to whom you're writing. This is the person who you want to actually open the envelope and read the letter you've folded inside. If you want to send a letter to someone in care of someone else's address, you need to write the person's name who you want to open the letter on the first line and, on the second line, write: c/o (this means "in care of") and the person's name whose address you're mailing it to. This person will take care of the envelope until it reaches the person for whom it's intended. The upper right-hand part of the envelope or package is where the stamp gets affixed. It looks like this:

Your Name
Your Street Address
Your City, State, and Zip Code

Stamp

To: The Name of the Intended Recipient
The Recipient's Street Address
The Recipient's City, State, and Zip Code

State and Territory Abbreviations

A specific state's abbreviation is fine, but it looks friendlier when the name is written out in its entirety. I can't be the only one to find state and territory abbreviations confusing. Especially states starting with M. And don't get me started on Alabama and Alaska. My friend Eric had a job as a rescue worker in Anchorage one winter. The first letter I sent him traveled all the way to Alabama and back before it finally reached his hands.

AL = Alabama

AK = Alaska

AZ = Arizona

AR = Arkansas

CA = California

CO = Colorado

CT = Connecticut

DE = Delaware

FL = Florida

GA = Georgia

HI = Hawaii

ID = Idaho

IL = Illinois

IN = Indiana

IA = Iowa

KS = Kansas

KY = Kentucky

LA = Louisiana

ME = Maine

MD = Maryland

MA = Massachusetts

MI = Michigan

MN = Minnesota

MS = Mississippi

MO = Missouri

MT = Montana

NE = Nebraska

NV = Nevada

NH = New Hampshire

NJ = New Jersey

NM = New Mexico

NY = New York

NC = North Carolina

ND = North Dakota

OH = Ohio

OK = Oklahoma

OR = Oregon

PA = Pennsylvania

RI = Rhode Island

SC = South Carolina

SD = South Dakota

TN = Tennessee

TX = Texas

UT = Utah

VT = Vermont

VA = Virginia

WA = Washington

WV = West Virginia

WI = Wisconsin

WY = Wyoming

TERRITORIES

AS = American Samoa

DC = District of Columbia

FM = Federated States of Micronesia

GU = Guam

MH = Marshall Islands

MP = Northern Mariana Islands

PW = Palau

PR = Puerto Rico

VI = Virgin Islands

Cynthia's Uncle Howie

"'Hi, how are you? I'm fine. Love, Cindy.' That's all I could write when I was six," my friend Cynthia laughs. Cynthia and I haven't seen each other in ten years and by chance have chosen the same vacation spot this summer. We're catching up over lunch in the stone dining room at Tassajara Zen Mountain Center in Carmel Valley, California, and talking about correspondence. Cynthia pours us each a glass of raspberry iced tea and confides that she and her Uncle Howie were pen pals when she was six.

"Uncle Howie always wrote back, even if he didn't really get how a six-year-old's mind worked," she recalls. He sent Cynthia long philosophical letters in response to her "Hi, how are you?" notes. She had no clue how to understand them, much less respond to her uncle's handwriting, but she adored the envelopes his letters arrived in. One in particular she describes as covered entirely with stamps from his collection. "You know, those one- and five-cent stamps?" Cynthia pauses, remembering the thrill of seeing that stamped-up envelope arrive with her name in large, adult-looking letters marching across the front from her beloved uncle in California. "I still have it, that envelope, next to my desk, and it still makes me happy every time I look at it." Cynthia smiles. "I love my Uncle Howie."

LETTER LEAD-IN

Write a letter to anyone under the age of ten today. Keep it simple, like the "Hi, how are you? I'm fine" variety. Make sure to cover the entire front of the envelope with one- and five-cent stamps, just like Uncle Howie did.

Put Enough Stamps on It

Molly de Vries owns a cool little textile shop called Ambatalia. It's located in an old shipping container where the local lumberyard used to be. Molly's a multigenerational Mill Valley resident and believes in selling only things that are nondisposable and that have a low impact on the earth, like her oversized furoshiki kitchen towels that can be used to carry groceries or worn as an apron. She makes and sells napkins and beeswax candles and pottery too. I walked Rasco down to see how the lumberyard's restoration into artist studios was going and to visit Molly today. She greeted us by showing me what she had received in the mail. "It arrived, just like this." Molly's eyes widened. "Without *any* packaging." On the windowsill sat an old lunchbox with stamps and a sticker marked "Fragile" affixed to the front. Molly's address and a U.S. Postal Service tracking number were painted in green letters and, along the side, the return address: Stinson Beach, CA (no zip code). "Go ahead, open it," Molly encouraged me. The inside was papered with French newsprint and a note in black watercolor: "Dear Molly, May this be the start of a long friendship. XO, B.J."

LETTER LEAD-IN

Using B.J.'s idea for inspiration, find an old lunchbox; paint it with the name and address of a new friend; leave a note inside; and if you mail it, be sure to stick on enough stamps and include the zip code.

Dear Reader,

At Camp Shaver, the YMCA summer camp I looked forward to every summer, we had songs for every occasion. Songs around the campfire, songs before meals, and songs for mail call—the rule was that when you got a letter, you had to get up and sing for everyone. While I remember the distinct thrill that receiving mail brought, I don't remember the exact day I got that letter from my mom, the one that I still have almost twenty years later.

Just after I graduated college, I lost my mother to a sudden death. One summer several years afterward, I was home for a visit, staying in my child-hood room, which had, at that point, remained largely untouched. In a bout of nostalgia, I opened the bottom drawer of my hand-painted dresser, which I had slowly piled full throughout my adolescence: triangle-folded notes written in the seventh grade, love letters from an eighth-grade boyfriend tied into a bundle with a pink scrunchy, letters from high school friends detailing summer adventures abroad.

I wasn't sure exactly what I was looking for, until I found it. A plain white envelope, addressed to Ava Dellaira, c/o YMCA Camp Shaver, Mountain Road Box 7, Jemez Springs, New Mexico. It was from my mom. She talked about how empty the house seemed with my sister and me away that summer, but how proud she was of the women we were becoming. It told us how much she loved us. It was signed with X's and O's, Mother Mary.

Since the day when I must have first carried the letter back to my cabin and read it atop a creaky bunk bed, the words have taken on new meaning, different weight. But the miracle of the letter is that every time I read it, my mom is still speaking to me, across all of that time and space.
Love,

Ava

Dear Kurt Cobain,

Mrs. Buster gave us our first assignment in English today, to write a letter to a dead person. As if the letter could reach you in heaven, or at the post office for ghosts. She probably meant for us to write to someone like a former president or something, but I need someone to talk to. I couldn't talk to a president. I can talk to you.

I wish you could tell me where you are now and why you left. You were my sister May's favorite musician. Since she's been gone, it's hard to be myself, because I don't know exactly who I am. But now that I've started high school, I need to figure it out really fast. Because I can tell that otherwise, I could drown here . . .

AVA DELLAIRA is a graduate of the Iowa Writers' Workshop. She grew up in Albuquerque, New Mexico, and received her undergraduate degree from the University of Chicago. She believes her novel *Love Letters to the Dead* began when she bought her second album ever—Nirvana's *In Utero*—which she listened to on repeat while filling the pages of her journal. She currently lives in Santa Monica, California, where she works in the film industry.

Include the Zip Code

Robert Moon, once a postal employee, is considered the father of the modern zip code (not that there's an ancient zip code). Unfortunately, though, the post office only gives Mr. Moon credit for the first three digits of the five-digit zip code. Sort of stingy, if you ask me.

ZIP is an acronym for Zone Improvement Plan. Zip codes officially arrived on the scene in 1963 as a way to help letters and postcards and packages "zip along" to their final destination, or zones, in the United States. Zip codes consist of five numbers—three of which we can thank Mr. Moon for, and two of which I'm not exactly sure who to thank for—that come after a person's city and state in an address. In 1980, an extra four digits were added to the original five to help the mail reach a specific zone with even more accuracy. "Zip plus four" is what they call it. (Mr. Moon, by the way, had nothing to do with *these* four digits.)

In the end, or close to it, zip codes aren't mandatory. But, hey, if they help your letter carrier get your letter or parcel (or even a lunch box like Molly's) to its destination quicker and make a postal worker's job easier, why not include them? There's a lot of mail out there to keep track of, and we don't want a letter to get lost and not reach its intended recipient. I'm sure Mr. Moon, wherever he is, would agree.

P.S. In England, Canada, and Australia, the zip code is called a "postal code."

WRITE TO DELIGHT

I traded messages with Paul Constant, a magazine writer, book editor, political reporter—and, it turns out, a spring roll–eating contest winner. (Full disclosure: I could have written him a letter but didn't have his snail mail address, so I e-mailed him.) I wrote to him about a poet we mutually admired named Kim-An Lieberman, thanking him for something startling and true that his words awakened in me. Soon after I hit the send button, Paul wrote back to thank me for finding the poetry of this woman who deserved a wider audience. A flurry of delight raced between our exchanges over Kim-An Lieberman's books, *Breaking the Map* and *Orbit*, and how we'd both worked at Borders Bookstore, once upon a time.

Here's what Paul initially wrote that touched me and must now be shared with you:

> *If you love something that somebody does—some art, some words, some sounds—you tell them that you love it. You tell everyone how much you love it, repeatedly and enthusiastically. Don't save your appreciation for later, or worry about wearing people out with your passion. Because the happy truth is this: if a piece of art truly moves you, you will never, ever run out of new adjectives to express how much you love it. Getting to love someone's art is one of the very finest parts of being alive.*

Some people are like works of art to me, especially writers who have rich inner worlds that they in turn share with us via words and images. When I remind myself of this, I think of some of my favorite writers: Elizabeth Gilbert, Gabrielle Zevin, Garth Stein, Cheryl Strayed, George Saunders, as well as all of the note-givers in this book. And the writers who are no longer with us, like Kim-An Lieberman.

LETTER LEAD-IN
Write to a few people who are like works of art to you. Write about a book they wrote or something they made with their hands that touched you.

Or just who they are. Even if you don't get anything back, make that reach and let them know how and why what they say or make affects you. Don't save your appreciation for later.

Summer on the Hudson

Years ago, when my son was four, we spent part of the summer with our friends Jill and Arno and their four children, Max, Josh, Lola, and Stella, in upstate New York. I wanted Collin to remember that summer, so I wrote him a letter. My intention was to give it to him one day when he was older. I found it recently and it sparked a lively conversation about what he was like as a toddler. "You were filled with intense joy and unrelenting exuberance," I told him, as he read about how, down at the river, Max and Josh showed him how to make a cave of his hands to catch fireflies, how he ran up the stone steps to show me and his dad. Collin read part of that letter out loud: "Last night you flung the screen door wide after dinner, your hair matted with sand, T-shirt stained green with pistachio ice cream. 'I love spittlebugs!' you screamed and then searched for the box turtle you'd found on our hike, the one you named Olive, immediately pressing your lips to her shell." He finished the letter and said, "Wow, I was a handful."

In writing him that letter, I see that I, too, wanted to imprint the world's exuberance on my heart—take that siren sound he made imitating fire trucks; swoop up that particular shake of his legs before he flipped into a swimming pool; package up all his passionate attempts to convince me why I had to let him stay up past his bedtime, so he could plunge through the dark with eyes open wide into another day, to seek out the hiding and charge headlong into his one amazing and evolving life.

LETTER LEAD-IN

Write a letter to someone younger than you, a child, your child, and tell him something you love about being in his life, sharing his journey. "C., You'll read this letter years from now and know I have enjoyed and will continue to enjoy every second of your growing-up years. I thank my lucky stars that I was the one chosen to ride along." Wait awhile to give it to him.

THE KINDEST THING

After a yoga class in downtown Ashland, Oregon, I was on my way to meet my family for brunch. At the corner of Main and Pioneer Streets, I stopped to wait for the green walking man sign, when a car rolled too far into the intersection. As I was planning my route around the large sedan, a man on the opposite corner with a white cane looked as if he was having trouble. The sidewalk, crowded with tourists and window-shoppers, was narrow and now this car was blocking the crosswalk. That man, alone in a sea of the sighted, was doing something with great concentration that most of us take for granted. That's when another pedestrian strolled up and with a great deal of respect said, "Hey, man, can I help you out? Here, take my arm." Happiness as bright as the summer sun surged up within me, witnessing this simple act of kindness.

Be vigilantly on the lookout for uplifting acts. What's the kindest thing you heard, overheard, saw, or observed today? The quietest, most authentic, gentlest? Write it on a slip of paper or jot it in a gratitude journal. Pull it out and read it the next time you're feeling blue.

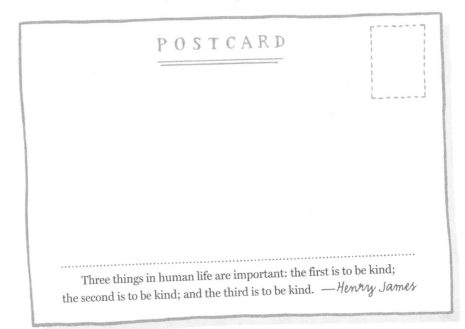

POSTCARD

Three things in human life are important: the first is to be kind; the second is to be kind; and the third is to be kind. —*Henry James*

Specific Days of the Year to Write

You can, of course, write off the following themes on the other 364 days of the year too. No one's stopping you.

TRIVIA DAY *(on or around January 4)*

Facts are great for starting conversations and winning at *Jeopardy*. Gather a few factoids and mail them to a friend on a postcard. Start with, "Hey, did you know . . . ?"

THESAURUS DAY *(on or around January 18)*

Make a list of favorite words—fewer than 920,000, the number the world's largest thesaurus contains—that express ways that you and a friend are similar.

NATIONAL HANDWRITING DAY *(on or around January 23)*

Start a writing marathon with a friend and challenge him to see who can collect more postmarks in the span of a month.

THANK A MAILMAN DAY *(on or around February 4)*

If you don't already know your mail carrier's name, find out. Then leave her a card for a change. Say how much you appreciate the letters she delivers. You needn't mention the bills.

DO A GROUCH A FAVOR DAY *(on or around February 16)*

Leave an anonymous note on your grouchiest neighbor's car windshield. Tell him that you hope he has his best day ever.

WHAT IF CATS AND DOGS HAD OPPOSABLE THUMBS DAY
(on or around March 3)

Write some note or poem of praise using the voice of your cat or dog, and send it to a human they particularly love. P.S. July 31 is Mutt's Day.

SAVE A SPIDER DAY *(on or around March 14)*

Copy your favorite passage from *Charlotte's Web* and mail it—or the entire paperback—to a friend. Include a few facts about the venerable predator.

POEM IN YOUR POCKET DAY *(on or around April 24)*

Recopy a poem, one of your own or one by a favorite poet, put it in your pocket, and give it away today.

LOST SOCK MEMORIAL DAY *(on or around May 9)*

Instead of tossing out a sock that's missing its pair, send it to a friend. Ask her to match it with a sock she's missing and to think of you when wearing them together.

REPEAT DAY *(on or around June 3)*

Celebrate something you do over and over again—brushing your teeth, making your bed, putting on your socks. Celebrate it again in writing as a warm-up.

COMPLIMENT YOUR MIRROR DAY *(on or around July 3)*

Come up with a mirror mantra, such as "Hello, Beautiful." Tape it to your mirror and tape a second copy on some random mirror out in the world.

HAPPINESS HAPPENS DAY *(on or around August 8)*

Admit when you're happy, and share this news with someone who you know genuinely wants you to be happy too.

RANDOM ACTS OF KINDNESS DAY *(on or around September 1)*

Do something kind for a friend or stranger for no reason: for instance, pay someone's toll, or leave a note rolled up with a rubber band for the person who delivers your newspaper.

FORTUNE COOKIE DAY *(on or around September 13)*

Make up a few fortunes of your own and tuck them into cookies. The cream-filled ones are particularly fun, though they can get kind of messy.

COLLECT ROCKS DAY *(on or around September 16)*

Write uplifting words on a variety of rocks with a Sharpie, put the rocks in a bowl, and leave it outside your front door with a note inviting people to take one.

WORLD HELLO DAY *(on or around November 21)*

Participate by penning ten "Hellos" and mention the day you're celebrating. Leave them in ten nearby mailboxes. Say "Hello" to ten or more people too.

ROOF OVER YOUR HEAD DAY *(on or around December 3)*

Look up. Remind yourself how lucky you are to have that roof over your head. Pen a list of the things you have to keep you warm, dry, safe, and comfortable.

CHOCOLATE-COVERED ANYTHING DAY *(on or around December 16)*

Put a small piece of chocolate in an envelope with one chocolaty sentence, and mail it to a friend. Or invite that person to meet you for dessert.

Dear Reader,

Writing by hand is a far more contemplative act than writing on a keyboard. I love shaping each letter of the alphabet, taking time to feel the language begin to take shape from my hand and mind, while my ear listens closely to what is being revealed and to its natural, variable rhythms. When body and mind are attuned, poetry—and letters—comes naturally.

Poets have been writing letter-poems for as long as there has been poetry in written form, and I have written quite a number of poems in the form of letters. Whether writing to a living poet or to one who has been dead for years—even centuries—they are confidential in tone but public in utterance. Hence, I've often talked about "long conversations with the dead," suggesting that the conversation of poetry is always contemporary.

—Sam

A SAMPLE OF SAM HAMILL'S TRANSLATION OF BUSON

By flowering pear
and by the lamp of the moon
she reads her letter

SAM HAMILL, one of the founders of Copper Canyon Press, is the author of more than a dozen collections of poetry, most recently *Habitation: Collected Poems*. He has also published several collections of essays and numerous translations, including *Crossing the Yellow River: 300 Poems from the Chinese*.

SMALL POEMS FOR EVERY SEASON

One of the most famous haiku poets was Kobayashi Issa, so there are many Issa "sites" in Japan. No, not websites but actual places where you can visit in person and see "haiku stones" engraved with his poems. Issa, who gave up the name Yataro when he was twenty-nine and began the new year as Issa (a name inspired by a single bubble in a cup of tea), is my and my editor's all-time favorite haiku writer. He wrote more than twenty thousand haiku and he held compassion for the smallest of creatures: fleas, flies, moths, mosquitoes. He was a master at observing ordinary life and the passage of time just as it was—the changing leaves, the falling snow—and revealing life's many layers of impermanence. Deeply committed to the temple of poetry, Issa took his craft seriously but never lost his sense of humor. He often kept company with and spoke directly to cats, snails, sparrows, even the persistent mosquito.

In honor of a favorite seasonal poem or your favorite haiku, write a few lines on a stone and leave it at a "site" where someone else can find and enjoy it, too.

POSTCARD

Mosquito at my ear, do you think I'm deaf? —*Issa*

Hang a Poetry Dispenser in Your Town

A Montana poet and writer Michele Corriel created the Poetry Dispenser. It looks a lot like a paper towel dispenser—you know, the metal kind that hangs in diner bathrooms next to the liquid pink soap. Only the Poetry Dispenser isn't filled with folded pieces of paper to dry your hands but rather with poems written by local poets of Bozeman, Montana, the town Michele now calls home. Dispensers live welded to metal poles on sidewalks and in lobbies, in museums and galleries, wherever poetry needs to appear. One visits the Bozeman Public Library; another one lives at the Pocatello Carnegie Library; and yet another travels around to different schools in the state via the Montana Humanities Project. Another lives in Michele's garage but has been known to show up during April for Poetry Month and other special literary occasions. The Poetry Dispenser has even appeared in Montana's state capital on Inauguration Day. Michele's brain buzzes with images and words, and she believes everyone should have a poem when they need one. She also has big plans for making sure this happens. More Poetry Dispensers are scheduled to pop up and include more poems from her poetry-popping friends. She plans to offer dispensers to other cities too. So keep an eye out as you're taking a stroll along your town's sidewalks. You just might find a poem waiting inside a paper towel dispenser for you to pull out.

Little Prayers, Lemons, and Love

My maternal grandmother, Nina Nelson—born Antonia Grandi—was the fourth of seven children in a large Sicilian family that immigrated from Palermo to Chicago to Oakland, California. Determined and brave, Nana, who stood five feet two inches, was a successful business owner and a generous soul. She used to climb a wooden ladder by her fence to poke lemons off her trees with the handle of a broom, then leave them in her mailbox for her gardener, Tony; she kept them in bowls in her sunny kitchen and used them to bake her signature lemon meringue pies, tart and sweet with stiff, perfectly browned, foamy peaks. She had a ritual of squeezing half a lemon into a cup of hot water every morning before carrying it like an offering into the living room, where she sat in her favorite chair to meditate and offer gratitude for her life's blessings. She offered up prayers while she cooked and walked and delivered meals to friends and strangers. She offered them while playing the piano, volunteering at the local food bank, and rubbing her granddaughters' feet while watching old movies.

When I'd drive down from San Francisco to visit her, she'd wait for me on her screened-in porch and stand on tiptoe to hug me hello, whispering how much she'd missed me. Before I'd leave, she'd always make sure to send me home with a shopping bag brimming with lemons and oranges— enough to give away to friends and to make several pitchers of fresh juice. All the small gestures she performed with great care remind me of how much she loved me and my sister. "More than tongue can tell," she'd write inside the notes and cards she sent to us, so we would never, ever forget.

LETTER LEAD-IN

Nana was the first person to teach me to thank the tree for giving its fruit. After we gathered lemons and oranges in her garden, she used to pat my hand and say, "my beautiful granddaughter," and lead me inside to eat. Who taught you to be thankful for something? Pass along some sentiment of thanks by offering a piece or a bowl of fruit to someone today, whether it's a friend or a not-yet-friend. Place a handwritten good day reminder with it.

LETTERS AND POEMS BECOME
SPICE SHIPS AND ORCHARDS

When I was a student of poetry in the MFA program at the University of San Francisco, I enrolled in a class taught by visiting poet Jane Hirshfield. Because most students that semester were focusing on fiction, only Maureen and I signed up for the poetry workshop. Rather than cancel the class, the director of the program asked Jane if we could meet informally at her house. Jane generously agreed, so each Sunday for eight weeks, I packed my satchel of poems and walked past the apple orchard at the bottom of my road and up the hill to Jane's. Her Border Collie Maggie met me and Maureen at the front gate, and the three of us walked through Jane's fragrant garden of lettuces and rosemary and sage to the kitchen door. I'll admit, it was pretty magical. After the class ended, the magic continued when Jane and I began a friendship of exchanged e-mails. When I asked if she'd contribute to this book, I was met by her innate generosity yet again, when she sent the following on ways that both letters and poems can become spice ships and orchards:

1. Think interesting thoughts. There's no reason to put pen to paper, really, except to invite yourself and someone else into a world that's richer than the one you step out of to enter words. Your words want to be at least as interesting as the actual world is, if the reader is going to stay inside them.

2. Make memorable music. When we speak, our heard voices carry some of the meaning—they rise when we ask a question, grow quiet in intimate moments. There's always a rhythm and tune to what we say on the page as well. Good writing happens when the ears are open.

3. Observe opulently. The deep time of writing gives you time to see in ways you might not be able to when rushing through the day in ordinary ways. Taking time to see sometimes more particularly and sometimes more imaginatively opens the cupboards of possibility and of feeling. When you describe anything—a cat, the weather—you are also always describing the state of your soul. And you are changing your soul's state as well, by the act of writing.

4. Allow strangeness. Writing a letter or poem is a zone of intimacy, freedom, and safety. It's a time to invite in thoughts and images and ways of saying that might seem odd or giddily foolish, even frightening; a place where the difficult emotions and the implausibly peculiar thought can each rise to the surface. You can always choose not to send the letter, not to publish the poem, or to erase whatever parts you want to later. But first, let your own fingerprints mark what you say; take the chance to say what only you and no one else would.

5. Discover new depths and dimensions. When you sit down to write a letter or a poem (anything beyond a grocery list, really), look for what's still undiscovered—within you, within the relationship, within the world. Take your attention into your hands and heart and pen with tenderness and fearless courage, shape it with attended-to words and music, and your letter will become like the lanterns and carpets of *The Arabian Nights.* They will unfasten themselves from inertness and come alive; they will ask you life's great questions: Where would you like to go next? How do you want to live? Wildly or tamely? Narrowly and plainly or inside the vast reaches of possibility, intensity, lavishness, and freedom?

Movement and Flowers along the Way

Movement is happening all the time. Tress sway, bees buzz, pens twirl over paper—life's a perpetual shimmery dance just waiting for us to take notice. I was moved by the doorbell yesterday, when a friend stopped by with a homemade dinner. I was moved again later when Owen, my ex-husband, surprised me with tickets to a play called *Fetch Clay, Make Man*, which I'd been wanting to see. After the play, I met Roxanne, a friend of my friend Barbara who builds tree houses for a living—and who has to hold on when the wind's moving and the trunk and branches sway. Roxanne told me how moved she was by the actor who had played Muhammad Ali. We got to talking about acting and writing and our hobbies, and Roxanne told me how she likes writing letters but keeps her envelopes unsealed as she makes her way down to the mailbox. "In case I see something along the way that I want to include," she explained. "I like to surprise a friend with something that grows near my front door. Like a flower or two." A few days later, I received a card from Roxanne with a photograph of some red peppers that had caught her eye while marketing. "Ah, nature's bounty," she wrote.

LETTER LEAD-IN

Sam Keen said, "Trust what moves you most deeply." Take notice of what moves you. One thing often leads to another. Keep your next letter to a friend unsealed and surprise yourself with what you find to include as you move down your path on your walk to the mailbox.

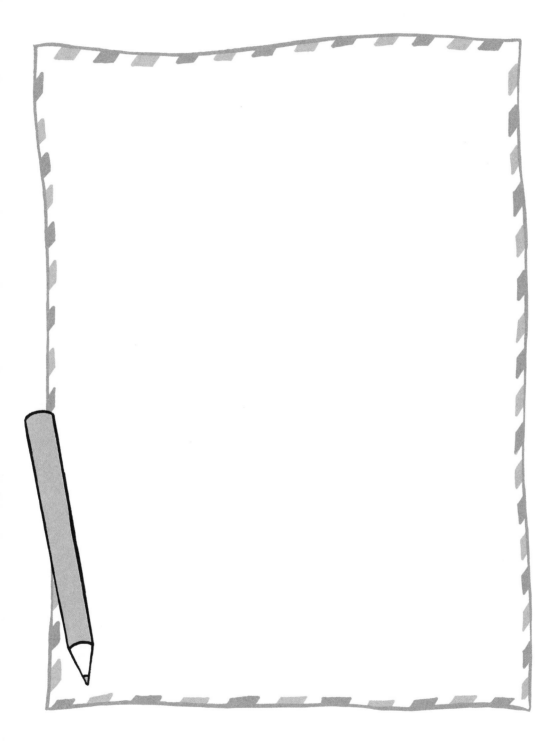

Hi, All.

It's a foggy day today at Muir Beach. I'm just back from a trip to the East Coast and soon will be off to other trips. It's been like this for me lately. I am surprised by this but so far so good. Many of my trips have been in support of the message of love and compassion, so I don't mind running around a bit to spread the word. Love is the only thing that really matters. As time goes on, I am more and more convinced of it. (If any of you have a better idea, let me know.)

Yours,

Norman

A SAMPLE OF NORMAN FISCHER'S WRITING

Here's a poem:

> unless language is
>   unless   it's   or you   were
>   a convenience , now   it's
>   shaped
>   as   the   way   a   ritual   is
>   in   time , according   to   words
>   that   do   not   mean
>   as   they   appear
>   stone , stone , river , river , tree
>   freedom , love , shame , shame , love
>   freedom, space , house
> as   is   or   that's   what   it   is . . .

ZOKETSU NORMAN FISCHER is a poet and Zen Buddhist priest. For many years, he has taught at the San Francisco Zen Center, where he served as co-abbot from 1995 to 2000. He is the founder and spiritual director of the Everyday Zen Foundation, an organization dedicated to adapting Zen Buddhist teachings to Western culture, and has often participated with the Beat Generation poets, especially Phil Whalen, Gary Snyder, and Michael McClure, his close friends and mentors.

Falling in Love through the Mail

Owen and I met at a tree-trimming party. We were both standing by the dessert table and began chatting over hot-spiced cider and a platter of star-shaped cookies. After we started dating, he sent me a letter every day. We lived a county apart, and those letters were what got me out of bed in the morning. Literally. I used to be a late-night writer, so sleeping in was mandatory. But the mail arrived by 10 A.M., and I didn't want to miss it. I'll explain. I lived in a cottage behind a house that belonged to a couple with whom I shared a mailbox. Sometimes the woman of the house would swoop all the mail out of that box and take it into her kitchen, and I'd have to wait two or three extra days—sometimes longer—for her to get around to bringing my mail down to me. To be fair, she worked full-time, had a child, and led a busy life. But I couldn't bear to wait. Anyone who knows me well will attest that I take receiving my mail soon after it arrives *very* seriously. I dreamed of having my own mailbox.

Luckily I could hear Patrick, my mail carrier, approaching with the chug and stop of his mail truck. So I'd throw off the covers, zip myself into my down jacket, and dash across the back lawn, up the stairs, and cross the driveway to arrive at that white mailbox shrouded in potato vines just as Patrick arrived. Out of breath, I'd greet Patrick, and he would respond, "Good day, Ms. Benke," in his old-world, gentleman-like way and promptly hand me my mail. This ritual would continue for the next fifteen years, even after I got married and moved up the hill, where my new house—with its very own mailbox—was included on Patrick's route.

Owen's letters arrived in light blue Par Avion (airmail) envelopes, were addressed in his sturdy cursive, and were filled with details of what he'd eaten for lunch and where he'd walked Scout, his Border Collie. They included descriptions of how much he missed me, how he was counting the days left in the work week until he could see me. I fell in love over his letters. I felt as if I'd met my letter-writing soul mate.

Through the smooth times and the not-so-smooth times, the simple act of receiving a letter is what offered us both connection, reassurance, solace, friendship.

LETTER LEAD-IN

Who delivers your mail? Who do you love receiving mail from? Here's encouragement to send a letter to the person who you see all the time. Maybe seal the envelope the old-fashioned way with wax.

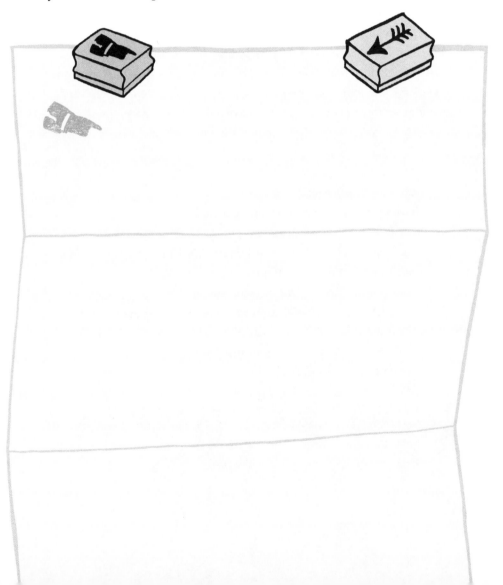

MAIL CARRIERS

Mail carrier and *letter carrier* are the official gender-neutral substitutes for *mailman*, since women deliver mail too. Sarah Black was the first woman mail carrier—her title was "mail messenger." In Australia, New Zealand, and Scotland, an employee of the post office is called a "postie." Up until 1916, U.S. mail carriers knocked on the doors of people's houses and waited for someone to answer. Though a polite gesture—Patrick used to walk packages down to my front door whenever it rained—you can well imagine how this could be incredibly inefficient. In fact, each mail carrier lost more than one and a half hours a day waiting for someone to answer the door! That's why the U.S. Post Office Department made it mandatory for every household to have a letter slot or a mailbox installed to continue receiving mail. Here are some famous people who were once real-life letter carriers:

Steve Carell, an American actor
Charles Bukowski, a novelist and poet
Peter Bonetti, an English goalkeeper
Paul Daniel "Ace" Frehley, an original guitarist for the rock band KISS
Keith Knox, a Scottish footballer
John Prine, a Grammy-winning folksinger
John Albert "Snowshoe" Thompson, who delivered mail on skis
Allan Smethurst, an English singer known as The Singing Postman
Ronald Belford "Bon" Scott, a former lead singer of AC/DC
Stephen Law, a philosopher

P.S. The oldest recorded mailbox in the United States is from the eighteenth century. Its current location is still on the corner of Boxtree Road and Lewis Road in East Quogue, New York.

Praise It, Don't Knock It

Unfortunately, it's easier to knock something than to praise it. Today, change that—even if you're feeling cranky and uninspired. Start by letting your mouth hunt for words that warm your heart. Then write a series of positive statements in the present tense that travel to all corners of the page. Reminder: it's the little things in life that matter. "October light streaming through the front windows. A chicken pot pie in the oven. Clive's bell warning the birds he's patrolling the garden again." Don't pay attention to your inner or outer critics. Don't give the cynics your attention. Watch out, some days they lurk everywhere! Instead, let grace and gratitude take you by the hands. Expend your energy by stringing positive images together like long rays of light or a whoosh of wind that blows your—and your cat's—hair back. Then watch how happiness expands. Fill an entire page. If a critical thought slips in, escort it right back out. As my friend Maria says, be willing to say these four powerful words: "Nevertheless, I am willing." If you're going to knock anything, let it be the door of a friend's house. When she looks to see who it is, invite her out for tea.

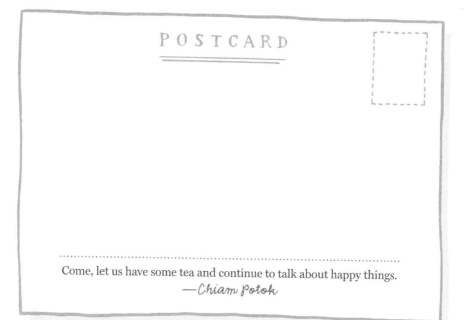

POSTCARD

Come, let us have some tea and continue to talk about happy things.
—*Chiam Potok*

My Letters' Return

My relationship with R. was ending. Fate had wielded a force stronger than either of us could fight against. Some of the gifts we'd exchanged over the years—carefully selected books, art objects, letters, quotes, poems—he had packed into cardboard and returned to my front porch. Each item, a reminder of a history we'd shared for half a decade. In the last patch of daylight, I sat on the chair we'd found at a yard sale and carried through wind and fog and up a flight of narrow stairs. I sat there, refusing to open that box, in disbelief of what we were now undoing. At last, I carried it inside and stacked each book on the floor, placing them largest to smallest. I took the paperweight he'd liked and could have kept but said was "too nice" and placed it on my windowsill along with the river stones we'd collected on one of our many hikes. Only then did I untie the ends of the indigo cloth that his hands had formed into a knot to hold the letters I'd written, photographs from our trip to Mexico one Christmas, a schedule from the day we sat in the Page Street Zendo—until all at once the tears I had not yet shed arrived, my pulse quickening as I felt myself falling into a place where words might no longer matter, the present changing right along with our future. It was then I knew I would have to learn this lesson of impermanence all over again, how loss and suffering course through each of us, penetrating every cell, touching all the moments lived separately, then together, and again separately. I loved him. He loved me. I left the letters at the bottom of that box from which they were returned, reminding my fragile heart how we're all just on loan to one another.

LETTER LEAD-IN

Re-read a letter you've received from a certain someone—or find a letter that has been given back to you for whatever reason. You might feel rejection, hurt, gratitude, relief, joy. If you decide to, write back to this person. You don't have to mail it.

Dear Reader,

On my desk are notes from the research I'm doing. My tea and teapot. Several pairs of reading glasses. Post-It notes. An ink pot and my fountain pen. OK, pens. I have several pens. I'm in New York, in the corner of my apartment, writing at a standing desk, which is an antique drafting table. There's a monitor on a shelf on the exposed brick wall in front of me, and above it loom four terrifying Mexican masks that I bought in Pátzcuaro, about 20 years ago, when I was there for the Día de los Muertos, the Day of the Dead, celebrations. They help me focus. Sometimes it's good to be reminded of one's mortality when one sits down to write. We can't escape the fact that we are beings with a time limit, but writing gives us a way of speaking across time. When we write, the past speaks through us as we cast our voices into the future.

As ever,

Ruth

A SAMPLE OF RUTH OZEKI'S WRITING
From *A Tale for the Time Being*

Print is predictable and impersonal, conveying information in a mechanical transaction with the reader's eye. Handwriting, by contrast, resists the eye, reveals its meaning slowly, and is as intimate as your skin. Ruth stared at the page. The purple words were mostly in English, with some Japanese characters scattered here and there, but her eye wasn't really taking in their meaning as much as a felt sense, murky and emotional, of the writer's presence. The fingers that had gripped the purple gel ink pen must have belonged to a girl, a teenager. Her handwriting, these loopy purple marks impressed onto the page, retained her moods and anxieties, and the moment Ruth laid eyes on the page, she knew without a doubt that the girl's fingertips were pink and moist, and that she had bitten her nails down to the quick.

Ruth looked more closely at the letters. They were round and a little bit sloppy (as now she imagined the girl must be, too), but they stood more or less upright and marched gamely across the page at a good clip, not in a hurry, but not dawdling, either. Sometimes at the end of a line, they crowded each other a little, like people jostling to get onto an elevator or into a subway car, just as the doors were closing. Ruth's curiosity was piqued. It was clearly a diary of some kind. She examined the cover again. Should she read it?

RUTH OZEKI has written four novels, including *A Tale for the Time Being*, a story told partly through the diary of a teenage girl in Japan and partly by a woman in British Columbia who finds the diary washed up on the shore after a tsunami. *A Tale for the Time Being* was short-listed for the United Kingdom's Man Booker Prize. Ruth Ozeki lives part-time in Canada and part-time in the United States.

EPISTOLARY IS NOT A DISEASE

I know it might sound like a disease of some sort, as in "Oh, she's suffering from a slight case of epistolary fatigue." But really, it's derived from the Latin word *epistola* by way of the Greek word *epistole*, both of which simply mean "a letter." For what we're after in this book, to encourage letter writing and note sending, it's a long word that has to do with letters, as in an "epistolary friendship."

There are also epistolary novels. These are novels written in the form of letters, diary entries, newspaper clippings, radio and blog posts, or even e-mails. Believe it or not, in the days before e-mail and text messaging, Twitter, Pinterest, Tumblr, and so forth, letters written by hand were a normal part of everyday life. Many authors embraced this form of communication, and a genre (form of writing) where the narrative is told in a series of letters was born. Some authors still write this way. Or they use letter writing as a warm-up before focusing on a novel, short story, poem, or play. For a partial list of epistolary novels, read on!

EPISTOLARY-RELATED BOOKS

People who know I like letters recommend epistolary-related books all the time. Just yesterday, Katie who works at the Mill Valley Library said, "Oh, you have to check out *Letters from a Nut* by Ted L. Nancy with an introduction by Jerry Seinfeld." So I did and I'm still laughing. Here's a starter list of some humorous and some series books written in the form of letters just for you.

Love, Mouserella by David Ezra Stein

The Day the Crayons Quit by Drew Daywalt; illustrations by Oliver Jeffers

Clementine's Letter by Sara Pennypacker; pictures by Marla Frazee

13 Little Blue Envelopes by Maureen Johnson

Letters to Leo by Amy Hest; illustrated by Julia Denos

Griffin & Sabine: An Extraordinary Correspondence by Nick Bantock

Why We Broke Up by Daniel Handler; art by Maira Kalman

The Perks of Being a Wallflower by Stephen Chbosky

The Guernsey Literary and Potato Peel Pie Society by Mary Ann Shaffer
   and Annie Barrows

Love Letters to the Dead by Ava Dellaira

The House I Loved by Tatiana de Rosnay

S. by J. J. Abrams and Doug Dorst

Super Sad True Love Story by Gary Shteyngart

Burley Cross Postbox Theft by Nicola Barker

A Visit from the Goon Squad by Jennifer Egan

Cloud Atlas by David Mitchell

The Lawgiver by Herman Wouk

Nothing But the Truth by Avi

Bridget Jones's Diary by Helen Fielding

Dracula by Bram Stoker

Poor Folk by Fyodor Dostoyevsky

The Moonstone by Wilkie Collins

Herzog by Saul Bellow

Carrie by Stephen King

Letters by John Barth

The Color Purple by Alice Walker

31 Letters & 13 Dreams by Richard Hugo

Birthday Letters by Ted Hughes

Floating Worlds: The Letters of Edward Gorey & Peter F. Neumeyer edited
    by Peter F. Neumeyer

The Letters of Emily Dickinson edited by Mabel Loomis Todd

F. Scott Fitzgerald: Letters to His Daughter edited by Andrew Turnbull

My Faraway One: Selected Letters of Georgia O'Keeffe & Alfred Stieglitz
    by Sarah Greenough

Dear George Clooney: Please Marry My Mom by Susin Nielson

DEAR YOUNGER/OLDER ME

I got this idea from *Dear Teen Me*, edited by E. Kristin Anderson and Miranda Kenneally, who asked seventy authors of young adult books to write letters to their teen selves. They were asked to write about things like who had a really bad or amazing first kiss, who skipped their prom to go to a Grateful Dead concert, and so on. What would *you* write to that fragile, angry, confused younger self, with the assurance and vantage point of having already lived through all that drama—thank God? What wisdom would you impart?

And what if you aren't yet or are still a teen? Then do what my seventh-grade English teacher, Mrs. Abe, asked of our class one rainy afternoon: write a letter on a piece of notebook paper about what's going on in your life right now. (I began by writing, "I'm sitting next to Nancy Salas, whose last name is a palindrone, and dreading my oral report on Sir Walter Raleigh.") Or write a few lines about what you currently love about your life, what you most appreciate. Seal what you write, address it to yourself, and keep it somewhere you can find it in ten years or give it to a close friend and ask her to mail it to you in a decade or two.

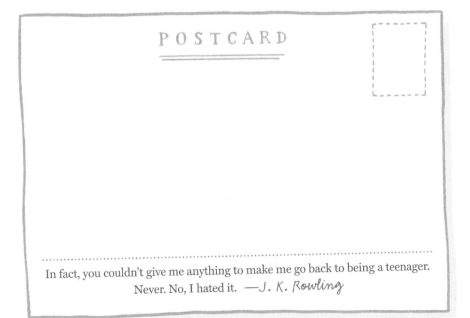

P O S T C A R D

In fact, you couldn't give me anything to make me go back to being a teenager. Never. No, I hated it. —*J. K. Rowling*

WHAT I KNEW AT SIXTEEN

At sixteen, I knew things I didn't yet have words for. One night, after a date with my boyfriend, I looked out the side window of the blue car he drove into a grove of trees between our neighborhoods. Out where horses grazed, we took a walk and kissed and kissed. I could taste the salt on his lips, feel his fine hair, hear his voice say my name in a whisper. Right there in the darkness lit by moonlight, I knew I would say good-bye to him forever. I'd have to. I would leave for college and let all that fitting-in energy fall away, to write in search of my future. I would travel the world and move closer to everything I would have to learn to attach words to, my life expanding at the very center, lit by the color of crushed pearls. There, in a Saturday night's luminescence, I stood gazing up, as I still do, at the same moon under which I continue to change, as I turn into a woman I have at last begun to recognize without deception or regret. This same pale light is what keeps me company as I awaken to everything I have always known but somehow forgot.

LETTER LEAD-IN

Write about something you're only just starting to find words for. Write it as a pep talk, say, for who you will be one day in the future. Think of the most understanding person you know as you write. Share this with that person.

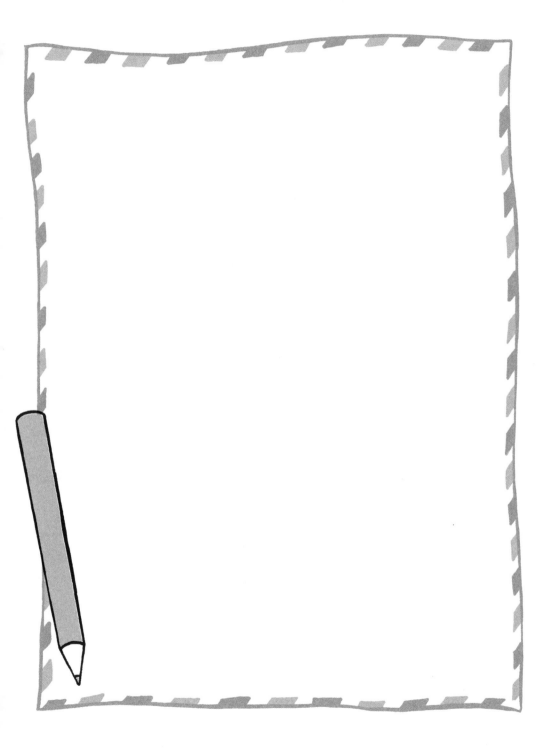

A NOTE IN A BOTTLE OR JAR

The next time you arrange to meet a friend for tea or a smoothie to talk, laugh, dish, and catch up on each other's lives, bring along some paper, a couple of pens, and an empty bottle or glass jar with a lid. On a loose-leaf sheet of paper (or across a paper napkin) compose a wish for the unknown person who will find it. Hope Anita Smith, a poet and author, gives out handmade notes and cards to strangers because it's something she genuinely enjoys. Her notes contain specific thank-yous. To a flight attendant she might pen an appreciation for their service and care—for that safety belt talk and extra blanket. She believes it's the simple acts we do for people that have huge impact.

Consider what you would tell someone you've never met. "You're fine just as you are." "Wander in wonder." Invite this person to pass a wish of his own forward, to keep the chain message in the roving bottle or jar moving from hand to hand, to different locations, to be found by another keen-eyed person who walks at a slower pace and takes notice of small-sized wonders. Include the date and your location, then sign off with your first names—or maybe with your pseudonyms.

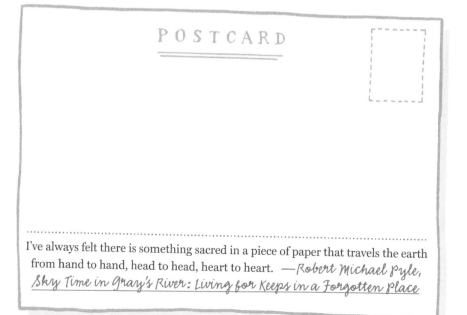

POSTCARD

I've always felt there is something sacred in a piece of paper that travels the earth from hand to hand, head to head, heart to heart. —*Robert Michael Pyle, Sky Time in Gray's River: Living for Keeps in a Forgotten Place*

Places to Write a Note or Pen a Letter

I used to think I had to have the perfect office setup in which to write, but after moving twice last year, I discovered that I can write just about anywhere. Sure, there are places I prefer more than others, but writing a letter—or a book—means that I'm writing *to* someone—like you—and when I'm with someone I care about in my heart, I find that I'm already home. Here's the start of my preferred places and situations in which to write. Pencil in your own.

On the window seat, aka Clive's napping spot
At Saru's Punjabi café
On my friend Tammara's porch (with Anna nearby)
In the warm glow of the Mill Valley Public Library
With Rasco Roon asleep at my feet
In the bleachers at Collin's basketball games
Next to the fireplace at Buck's cabin
While eating a bowl of cold cereal
Under a halo of lamplight late at night
In a tree house
Before yoga class
In Aida's garden
On my yellow couch
In Albert and Todd's poetry chair (made entirely of books)
Parked on Edgewood Avenue
After receiving good news
With a mug of hot chocolate
Wherever Collin's doing his homework
In my pajamas
On top of a mountain
As one hour sweeps into the next

A NOTE IN THE BATHROOM

When I was growing up, my father worked for Pacific Bell, otherwise known as The Telephone Company. His job involved climbing telephone poles, splicing wire, and repairing switchboards and telephone lines. At home, we had telephones in every room, even the bathroom. So did my Grandma and Grandpa Benke. At their house, there was a built-in shelf with a notepad and pen stored beneath where my father had installed a beige push-button phone in their guest bathroom. "If someone calls while you're on the pot, for god's sake, Sam, take a message!" Grandma Benke would holler. Sam, my grandpa, was a patient man with a sense of humor, who liked to pretend he couldn't hear what Grandma was hollering, to make his grandchildren laugh. (We did.)

I made sure to leave a note by that beige phone in the beige bathroom whenever I visited. I loved imagining Sam and Betty (their real names, I was thrilled to write) finding my notes after I'd gone home. It became a game between us. Sometimes I expanded my random note leaving to messages hidden beneath their pillows, tucked inside coat pockets, and poking up from the toaster. But my favorite place remained that small shelf next to the phone in that beige bathroom with velvet striped wallpaper, fluffy monogrammed towels, a pad of stationery with Alum Rock Realty stamped on the front, and a ballpoint pen that Grandma got after Grandpa to return whenever it went missing. "Sam!"

LETTER LEAD-IN

Leave five hidden notes for someone you know. In what five places will you leave them?

Dear Reader,

I think my favorite letters I've ever received were from my granny. When I was growing up, I lived near her, so no letters were necessary, but whenever I went away, she would write me dutifully and tell me all her news: what she'd eaten for lunch, what the neighbor's dog was up to, that kind of stuff. It should've been boring, but I loved how it took me into her world. But my favorite thing about her letters was the way she signed them, always with a long acronym of some kind. She was fond of T.T.F.N., which stood for Ta Ta For Now. She was a very funny lady, and as she came to the end of her life, her acronyms got sort of dark. She'd sign off "O.B.T., Granny." O.B.T. stood for On Borrowed Time. Or N.L.F.T.W. for Not Long For This World. I loved that she invented her own secret code. I still have a few of her letters and feel a surge of love whenever I see her spidery handwriting.

—Claire

A SAMPLE OF CLAIRE DEDERER'S WRITING
From *Poser: My Life in Twenty-Three Yoga Poses*

I wasn't my mom. I was hidebound by my need for security. But somehow I had made this leap, just this little leap, with my family, across the country. Now here we were, all together, dazed and happy. We'd done it!

Events are not what make up family life. Family life exists in the nonevents: the meals, the arguments, the reading together, the backyard soccer, the getting ready for school. We hid alone together on our mountain and reveled in the nonevents. Bruce and I had a bedroom at the top of the house, three stories up, where you felt like your forehead was grazing eight thousand feet. (Coloradans are obsessed with the metrics of altitude.) The room was huge and airy and mostly made of glass; it shook in the thirty-mile-an-hour winds that scoured the mountaintop. In that high room, there was a high bed. Bruce is six four; the mattress was at his chest height. We needed stairs to get in.

A Saturday afternoon: No one wants to drive up or down the mountain for a playdate. The family is aboard, about, above, across the bed, with comic books and radios, with arguments and elbows to nose. Willie creates an obstacle course, leaping off the bed onto various cushions. Lucy reads *Harry Potter* and listens to *Wait Wait . . . Don't Tell Me!* at the same time, while riding the exercise bike next to the bed. I fold laundry. Bruce spends some time debating with himself about what he should eat next.

CLAIRE DEDERER is the author of the best-selling memoir *Poser: My Life in Twenty-Three Yoga Poses*. She gets a thrill when she receives a hand-addressed letter and is especially happy if there are drawings on the envelope.

Lea Redmond is a postmaster at the world's smallest post office located in Berkeley, California, where she works out of Leafcutter Studio. Lea sends small—and I'm talking teeny-tiny—letters inside itty-bitty envelopes. Letters from Santa and the Tooth Fairy, marriage proposals—every imaginable kind of small, magical everyday notes that people ask her to write and mail for them. And tiny gifts too. She ships them all over the world with her brother Devin's help, in large padded envelopes, since the smallest size envelope the U.S. Postal Service will accept is 3½ × 5 inches (FYI, if your letter is smaller than that, it will be returned to you).

Lea's an artist and has created the tiny do-it-yourself World's Smallest Post Service activity kit, in case you want to make super tiny letters with super tiny fine-tipped pens and stamps and miniature envelopes to prove the best things in life really do come in small packages. There are even tiny Handle with Care, Special Delivery, and Air Mail stickers. Lea makes organic cotton notebook "paper" too, so you can embroider your letter or poem or quote with a needle and colored thread for a favorite friend.

But the best thing about the Leafcutter Studio operation is that you can visit Lea's miniature post office in Berkeley. It's tucked into the knothole of a tree on the Curran Trail in Tilden Park. The desk, lamp, chair, typewriter, and mini post office are an ode to all things small. Her post office is also stocked with miniature letters for you to take home. People who visit often leave tiny letters too, even though the office is made for those the size of a field mouse or butterfly. Hikers with names like Penelope and Freddie leave letters. Simply use the small map Lea provides on her website as a guide.

SOME POSTAGE REQUIRED

Postmaster Lea
Leafcutter Designs
1528 6th Street
Berkeley, CA 94710
www.leafcutterdesigns.com

A Small Story for a Small Person

My five-year-old friend Anna likes to get reacquainted by sitting side by side and reading her newest favorite picture book. One of our favorite authors is Cynthia Rylant, and we especially love her early-reader series about Henry and his good dog, Mudge. Today Anna and I are on her front porch eating Cheerios minus milk from a blue bowl and breathing in the sweetness of the afternoon, when I mention that the reason I like Cynthia Rylant's books is because of the snappy dialogue. "Yes, I know," Anna agrees, resting her hand on mine. "And how Mudge likes to get dirty." We're about to start the story about Mudge going to obedience school, when Anna tosses a few Cheerios across the sidewalk. When I copy her, she gives me one of her Anna-friendly shoves, then tosses the rest of the bowl over and throws her head back and laughs. I laugh too. Then we lean in close to read, while a family of birds enjoys our cereal snack.

Send a favorite passage from a picture book to a young friend, or mail the entire book with an invitation to sit side by side and read out loud. Inscribe the book, so your friend can remember it was from you.

POSTCARD

I love the rebelliousness of snail mail, and I love anything that can arrive with a postage stamp. There's something about that person's breath and the hands on the letter. —*Diane Lane*

Adjectives for Your Nouns

Adjectives are, as you probably know, descriptive words that modify nouns. (I include the definition here, since sometimes *I* forget.) The trick with using adjectives well is to remember the old adage, "quality, not quantity." Piled-up adjectives can spoil a good sentence. When you find just the right adjective for the job, though, go ahead and use it. Think precision when you select your adjective. Here's a starter list for you to continue:

splendid   wonderful   fantastic   clever   pretty   zany

comfortable   valuable   worthy   important   angelic

lovely   amazing   surprising   radiant   unusual   dreamy

uplifting   happy   gleaming   everlasting   shining   glowing

carefree   balanced   excited   outgoing   funny

quick-witted   blissful   upbeat   elated   sweet   soft

silent   vociferous   thunderous   inventive   whispered

hushed   jocular   shimmering   munificent   clownish   tasty

delicious   savory   lavish   delectable   serene   yummy

luscious   luminous   appetizing   spicy   silky   sensitive attractive   velvety   polished   zealous   willowy

lean   aromatic   voracious   fragrant   scented   bustling

sweet-smelling   jesting   snappy   swift   sizzling   full

open   playful   light   redolent   bright   swinging . . .

The Boy with Red Hair

Last spring, Annie asked if I'd come write poems with her fourth- and fifth-grade class. I wasn't sure if I still had the knack to engage a large group of kids, having worked the previous semester with older adult-kids. But I agreed, prepared, and arrived during their language arts hour. It turned out to be one of those classroom visits where I needed to say very little, since the poem I'd chosen by Pablo Neruda immediately got everyone excited to pick up a pencil and write. After a while, a boy with red hair motioned me over, said my name without looking up, and with all his freckles mustered the courage to ask if I'd take his poems home, read them, and write to tell him what I thought. I glanced at the clock, then back to his pleading eyes. "Sure," I answered. So he copied down his address, and I tucked his poems into my bag. "You promise?" he asked again, before I stepped outside to chat with Annie. I nodded, "I promise."

Over the years, I've been asked by writers young and old if I'll read what they've written, tell them what I think. I make my living by writing and by editing other people's work, by encouraging them so they will share their words with a wider audience, too. But I also have to charge for my time to pay my rent, buy groceries, keep the electricity on so I can see to read at night. I wouldn't ask a doctor I met at a party, "Hey, could you take a look at this mole and tell me if I should have it removed?" But there was something about that boy, the urgency with which he wrote, that made me say yes to his request. When I wrote back, I gave him a praise sandwich: I started with everything I liked about his poems; then mentioned a few things I didn't understand or wished there was more or less of; and ended by thanking him for his trust in me, for giving me the chance to know him through his writing. And for being so brave.

LETTER LEAD-IN

Write an opinion letter to a friend or acquaintance, starting with "Here's everything I liked or loved about . . ." Whatever your opinion, write a praise sandwich.

P.S. Consider joining a writing group—or gather a few friends who like to write and start one of your own. This can be a helpful way to learn how your words are heard and understood. A writing group can be formed in person or through letters.

WRITING IN PAIRS

Maggie asks if she spelled *fair* right, as in, "Not fair, Jack. I raised my hand first." She says she doesn't care about where pigs win ribbons. "Fair is fare, and you know it, Jack!" Maggie is nine and has definite ideas about how classroom rules should operate. I respect this. Today, I'm the visiting poet. I look into the sea of third-grade faces, their flung backpacks and wiggly bodies, and ask who likes to write letters. That's when Drake says he's got the word *dread* stuck in the middle of his head, and Kyle, across the aisle, opens a bag of pretzels and challenges Eli to untwist one. I ask who knows how to handwrite, and Sam passes his eraser to Emma. Emma raises her hand and declares that she can write in cursive, "See?" She holds up her paper of smudged printed letters connected with little kickstands and swirls to make them all connect along the bottom. Sam asks Emma if he can borrow his eraser back. Maggie tells Jack not to say another word to her today, "thank you very much." Playground sounds drift down the hall. About to clap for them to listen and demand their attention, I close the door instead and revel in this wayward chorus: twenty hearts, various voices, the morning I slogged through to arrive today suddenly refocused. Soon, we all have a writing pal and are penning our letter-poems. Even Maggie and Jack. It all works out. It always does. Only not exactly the way I had planned.

Venture to ask a new friend to be your writing pal. Make a writing date, bring a notebook, and meet up with a bag of pretzels.

I like a teacher who gives you something to take home to think about besides homework. —*Lily Tomlin*

ANNIVERSARY OF A FRIEND'S DEATH

I stand at the whiteboard where Dee, my friend who taught for over thirty years at Park Elementary School, once stood. I share with the class how the stream wouldn't have a song if it weren't for the rocks. I ask who has their own rock collection, and many hands shoot up. Everyone loves rocks. I hold up one of my favorites, and they tell me what they see: "That one looks like a dog with ginormous spots." "No, it's the Earth spinning. Watch, like this," a boy in front insists. I place a rock on every desk. "That's a spaceship, rescuing a planet on fire," a girl states as a fact. They toss stray questions my way: "So we can write about *anything*?" I imagine Dee, leaning down to listen to the universe of these eight-year-olds. She taught her students to recite Shakespeare and to perform their poems of rocky wildness slowly, to enunciate to the back row: "My rock becomes a sparrow, sun for wings, feathers for flight." "Mine's a lost memory unwinding through a bend in time." Everyone wants a chance to read. After the bell, I gather their images and walk down the hall, remembering their voices, the way Dee smiled, nodding her head, my collection of rocks alive again from the attention of so many hands.

LETTER LEAD-IN

Write about small things you remember a loved one touching—doorknobs, spoons, letters, rocks. Write about how she touched you. Then send it to that person. Or, if she's gone, send it to someone still living who knew and loved her too.

Everyday Shakespeare to Start or End a Letter

Add your own twist to personalize some of Will's famous sayings by adding phrases such as "You are," "Let's," "It's a," "It's been," "I am," and so on. I've given you examples for the first few.

Forever and a day (It's been forever and a day!)
Break the ice (Okay, let's break the ice.)
Brave new world (It's a brave new world.)
Play fast and loose
The world's my oyster
Sweets to the sweet
Full circle
Wild-goose chase
Melted into thin air
One fell swoop
Primrose path
Set my teeth on edge
Foregone conclusion
Bated breath
Kill with kindness
Tower of strength
What the dickens
Seen better days
Sick at heart
What's done is done

What You Taught Me

As a shy nine-year-old, I was inspired by Marcia Donnelly, my fourth-grade teacher at Linda Vista Elementary School in San Jose, California. It was Mrs. Donnelly who read *Stuart Little* out loud to us and who taught our class the lyrics of "Bad Bad Leroy Brown," "Copacabana," "The 59th Street Bridge Song (Feelin' Groovy)," and a few dozen other songs. After lunch, Mrs. D. would push back her light blonde shoulder-length hair and, in her Swedish accent, ask the room monitors to please raise the blinds, turn off the fluorescents, and bring her guitar up from the back of the room. With song lyric folders open and the sun streaming through the tall windows that looked onto the playing field, we'd begin singing.

I put everything I kept hidden inside my heart into the songs we sang, all the shyness and excitement, wonder and magic that swirled through me. I felt safe and free, watching the pine trees in the field above the school blow in the wind, singing those happy, reassuring lyrics. That hour after lunch has stayed with me for decades, as did the way Mrs. Donnelly strummed her guitar, encouraging us; how she gave a shy girl a chance to break free and feel special to herself (even groovy) for a while.

LETTER LEAD-IN

Who taught you to love something? Write to that teacher and say so: "Dear Mrs. Donnelly, Because of you, I break into spontaneous song." "Dear Ms. Gambetta, Because of you, I love traveling to Ashland for the Shakespearean Festival." "Dear Gary Thompson, Because of you, I write poems and stop to admire the yellow leaves of gingko trees."

P.S. Send your letter on National Teacher Appreciation Day, which falls on the Tuesday in the first full week of May.

Dear Reader,

I love letters! Getting a letter is like getting a birthday or Christmas or Chanukah gift that might arrive any day of the year. Letters make me feel special because someone has taken the trouble to write something just for *me*. As soon as I hear my mail drop through the slot by my front door, I rush to collect it and look for letters. Most of my mail consists of advertisements, catalogs, and bills. No fun! I put all of this stuff aside on the buffet in my entry hall and look for letters. Finding one, I take it to a comfortable chair where I can read and enjoy it. I especially like hearing about my friends' family news and their travel to exotic places. I never throw letters away but keep them forever in boxes and files.

My poem "Letter to Send in a Space Capsule" is a different sort of letter. It's addressed to intelligent beings elsewhere in the universe, millions of years in the future. I wrote it fearing what pollution, global warming, and possible future wars might do to the planet Earth. In this letter, I express the hope that the Earth as we know it will still exist in the distant future. Another of my poems, "Chain Letter," was made into a children's book. This poem makes fun of chain letters because I think they're silly.

Your friend,

Lucille Lang Day

A SAMPLE OF LUCILLE LANG DAY'S WRITING

Excerpt from "Letter to Send in a Space Capsule"

I lived on the third planet circling an ordinary star
at the edge of a spiral galaxy two million light-years
from the Andromeda Nebula. We called it Earth.
In spring the mock cherry trees were flocked
with white blossoms when maples blazed green

and hummingbirds with long, narrow beaks
and brilliant throats sucked nectar
from red and orange flowers. In summer
the sky was pale blue and sometimes feathered
with clouds like the wings of giant swans.

LUCILLE LANG DAY is the author of eight poetry collections and chapbooks, most recently *The Curvature of Blue*. She has also published a children's book, *Chain Letter*, and a memoir, *Married at Fourteen*, which received a 2013 PEN Oakland Josephine Miles Literary Award. Her poems, essays, and short stories have appeared widely in magazines and anthologies.

A Note Slid under the Door

I was fortunate to be given a month-long writing residency on Whidbey Island one winter. So I put my mail on "hold," locked the door of that cottage tucked behind the house owned by the couple with whom I shared the mailbox, and flew up to Langley, Washington, to a place called Hedgebrook. Created by the philanthropist Nancy Nordoff, Hedgebrook is a haven for women writers of all genres, from all over the world. Scattered over forty-eight acres, with views across Puget Sound to Mount Rainier, are six cottages crafted in the "post-and-beam" style where six women are invited to write from one week to three months. The cottages are situated so that each writer can see the light of another cottage through the trees at night; so she can write in solitude but also feel a part of a community, knowing each light represents a woman inside with paper and pen. A large farmhouse with a welcoming kitchen is also on the property, where a chef makes the residents' meals and the cookie jar is never empty.

I was assigned to Owl Cottage, across from the shed of split alder and next to a waterfall by a path that leads to the lake. A sloped roof covered me as I ventured into the depths of my heart, during those long, quiet hours at my desk by the window. Every morning I'd build my own fire, establishing trust in my own resourcefulness, and every afternoon I'd find a lunch basket of soup and bread and homemade cookies (from that never-ending jar) left at my doorstep. It was here I learned I could also let others care for me as I worked. It was here sunlight seeped through stained glass to find me putting word after word onto the clean page of winter.

After dinner around the pine table, the six of us would walk the gravel road back, wishing one another a good night as we splintered off in the direction of our cottages. The last two writers were always me and Sandy Diamond, a poet, playwright, and calligrapher, who told the best stories as we waded deeper into the night of stars pressed high in the January sky. A bullfrog croaked his tired song as cattails bent into the wind, and the light from Sandy's and my flashlights crisscrossed, illuminating the fork where our paths diverged. Once inside Owl Cottage, I'd climb the stairs to the loft and write in the Owl guest journal, and later dream of my life in the form of small poems. I'd often wake to find an unsealed note slid underneath my front door from Sandy who, in her fine handwriting, would wish me a productive day, call me the darling of Hedgebrook, and ask if I'd swing by and pick her up later on my way to dinner.

LETTER LEAD-IN

Slide a note under someone's door, wish her a productive day, and ask her to join you later for a walk somewhere or out to dinner. Oh, and don't forget your flashlights.

Send Yourself a Postcard

Collin and I took a road trip last week to Santa Cruz, to visit my sister and brother-in-law, aka Tia and Uncle Brad. We packed the VW with snacks and Kathryn Stockett's book *The Help* on CD (all fourteen disks). We stopped once for a bathroom break, when I had to hike into a field because someone had locked the gas station's bathroom door, then driven off with the key. "It was the only key we had," the attendant explained. "Guess it's the field for you, Mom," Collin laughed. Otherwise we drove and munched and listened and were transported back to Mississippi of 1963. When we arrived in Santa Cruz, we said our hellos to Tia and Uncle Brad, then Collin made a beeline to see Larry, the boa constrictor who lives in the office, while I sat on the carpet and made a fuss over Vanna and Lola, the cats.

The next day, after breakfast, we walked around downtown where I found a shop with sendable gifts—envelope-sized giraffe key chains (with bendable necks), miniature decks of cards, chocolates wrapped in literary quotes—plus an entire wall of stationery and a counter where customers can stand and write postcards. I was thrilled; Collin, less so. He ducked out to visit the surf shop next door while I penned postcards to friends and then wrote one to myself, a reminder of our mother-son road trip—how Brad barbecued chicken, how my sister put extra blankets in the guest room and suggested I lock the door if I was that scared Larry might take a midnight slither. Before we left, we bought more snacks and decided on the coastal route home. We paused *The Help* to show off our southern accents and stopped for just-picked strawberries at a roadside stand.

I tend to forget the details of life unless I write them down, and I *love* the details: the cows grazing the hills above Half Moon Bay, Collin resting his head out the window, wind rippling through his brown hair. So much is constantly happening, all at the same time. Thankfully we can uncap a pen to slow it all down. Later in the week, after collecting the mail, Collin wandered into the living room and dropped a postcard in my lap. "Hey, Mom, who sent you this?"

LETTER LEAD-IN

Next road trip, write yourself a postcard as an act against forgetting. Dash out original details from your original life. It's a souvenir from your hands to your heart in the familiarity of your own handwriting.

Hello from Peace Rally City

I received a short letter from my friend Kat, just back from a peace rally with her young daughter. In a small amount of space, she'd written a description of their afternoon in vivid detail: her daughter asleep, wrapped in a tie-dyed blanket; the woman standing next to her with whom she'd exchanged pleasantries and who wore lines of the sleep-deprived under her eyes too. Kat wrote how she could tell this woman understood the world's suffering, how we must continue to celebrate birthdays, pretend to love Santa Claus, and keep spooning applesauce into our children's hungry mouths, all while refusing to let fear rule.

That short letter allowed me a glimpse into my friend's day and heart and life, her concerns for a world that sometimes looks as if it has gone crazy, and how she doesn't always know what else to do except write letters to Congress and volunteer and take part in peaceful protests. She adores her sweet daughter and wants her to inherit a better, more generous world. In a few well-chosen lines, I could see my friend raising her sign smudged blue with Magic Marker a little higher, as sunlight peeked through cracks of a December sky. I could hear those cars honking into the hub of a busy intersection during a Saturday morning rally for peace.

LETTER LEAD-IN

Begin a letter back to a friend whose letters you love to receive and tell him all the small details of something you recently did with a group of people: "Your letter arrives as the heliotrope bends into morning, the wisteria is about to bloom again . . . a pack of teenage boys scattered through the living room, in sleeping bags, soon to wake and request massive amounts of pancakes . . ."

WORDS THAT RHYME WITH POSTMARK

Postmarks are made by hand or by a machine, depending on the post office. Hawaii Post has a rubber-stamp postmark that was once a hand-painted surfboard. A postmark is a marking—like that surfboard—that indicates the date and time the letter, postcard, or parcel was delivered into the post office's care. Modern postmarks are often applied at the same time as the cancellation mark, those wavy lines used to cancel a stamp so it can't be used again. *Marcophily* is the study of postmarks. There are even clubs that meet to share the hobby of collecting postmarks. In the United States, The Post Mark Collector's Club was founded in 1946. Depending on how rare or attractive they are, certain postmarks bring more value to the stamps, so make sure you choose carefully.

In case you're ever in a rhyming mood while writing a letter, or want to impress a postal worker while you're waiting for your packages to be processed—and the line behind you isn't too long—here's an alphabetized list of thirty-two words that rhyme with *postmark*:

aardvark   airpark   anarch   ballpark   benchmark

birthmark   bookmark   check mark   debark   Denmark

earmark   footmark   hallmark   horned lark   landmark

monarch   Petrarch   pitch arc   Plutarch   pockmark

pork chop   pressmark   remark   ringbark   seamark

skylark   space mark   tanbark   theme park   tidemark

trademark   white shark

If a letter is being sent by air—*par avion* (literally "by airplane" in French)—a special blue sticker label is used. The official language of the Universal Postal Union is French, so that's why you see it written both in French and in a country's home language (*airmail* in the case of the United States). There are specially marked envelopes and special airmail stamps available—or required—depending on the country your letter is being sent from. *Aerophilately* is the study of airmail, in case you want to learn more.

P.S. *Parcel post* is a postal service term for mail that's too heavy or too wide to qualify for normal letter post. It's often slower than letter post too. There's also express (the fastest) and media mail (my favorite) for when you're sending books.

The Places You Will Go

Some people travel for traveling's sake. Others travel for inspiration, to pass through doorways of discovery, to simply get to a set destination, to escape, or to find themselves anew. We all dream of going to places we've never been. (At least I hope we do.) On the back of a postcard, write the names of a few of your want-to-see-one-day places. Address the postcard to your most adventurous friend, ask him to circle the location he likes best, and invite him to come with you. It doesn't matter if you write on the back of a lake or city skyline or an island at sunset. No need to say "wish you were here." Simply gaze out the window and imagine your invitation being received with a smile. You must dream big before big trips can happen. Within five minutes, affix a postcard stamp, if mailing from and to somewhere in the United States, and send it on its way. Maybe you'll mail postcards to a few friends, or create a homemade passport to offer yourself and a friend even more opportunities to visit places in the world you want to add to your bucket list. Turn the page for travel location suggestions.

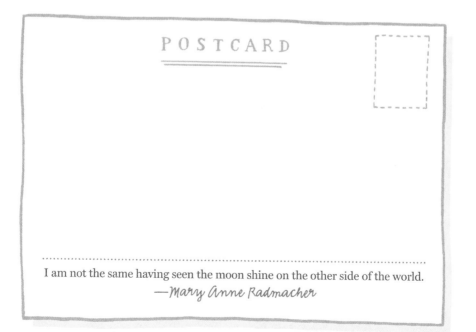

POSTCARD

I am not the same having seen the moon shine on the other side of the world.
—Mary Anne Radmacher

Countries of the World

The world is vast yet continually shrinking, especially with regard to how fast we can communicate with one another. Today, e-mail the friend who lives the farthest distance away from you and let her know that a letter's on its way. Then keep your word and write it. It's fun to anticipate a letter's arrival. If you're inclined, figure out which twenty-five countries are missing from the following list. Or find a pen pal from a different country you're interested in visiting.

Afghanistan	Bolivia	Czech Republic
Albania	Botswana	Denmark
Algeria	Brazil	Djibouti
Anguilla	Brunei Darussalam	Dominica
Antarctica	Bulgaria	East Timor
Antigua	Burkina Faso	Ecuador
Argentina	Burundi	Egypt
Armenia	Cambodia	El Salvador
Aruba	Cameroon	Eritrea
Australia	Canada	Estonia
Austria	Cape Verde	Ethiopia
Azerbaijan	Cayman Islands	Faeroe Islands
Bahamas	Chad	Fiji
Bahrain	Chile	Finland
Bangladesh	China	France
Barbados	Christmas Islands	Gabon
Barbuda	Colombia	Gambia
Belarus	Congo	Georgia
Belgium	Cook Islands	Germany
Belize	Costa Rica	Ghana
Benin	Croatia	Gibraltar
Bermuda	Cuba	Greece
Bhutan	Cyprus	Greenland

Grenada
Guadeloupe
Guam
Guatemala
Guinea
Guyana
Haiti
Honduras
Hungary
Iceland
India
Indonesia
Iran
Iraq
Ireland
Israel
Italy
Ivory Coast
Jamaica
Japan
Jordan
Kazakhstan
Kenya
Korea
Kuwait
Laos
Latvia
Lebanon
Liberia
Liechtenstein
Luxembourg
Macedonia
Madagascar

Maldives
Mali
Marshall Islands
Martinique
Mexico
Monaco
Montenegro
Montserrat
Morocco
Mozambique
Namibia
Nepal
Netherlands
New Zealand
Nicaragua
Niger
Nigeria
Norway
Oman
Pakistan
Panama
Papua New Guinea
Paraguay
Peru
Philippines
Poland
Portugal
Puerto Rico
Qatar
Romania
Rwanda
Saint Lucia
Samoa

Saudi Arabia
Senegal
Serbia
Seychelles
Sierra Leone
Singapore
Slovenia
South Africa
Spain
Sri Lanka
Sudan
Sweden
Switzerland
Tajikistan
Thailand
Tonga
Tunisia
Turkey
Uganda
Ukraine
United Kingdom
United States
Uruguay
Uzbekistan
Vanuatu
Venezuela
Vietnam
Virgin Islands
Western Sahara
Yeman
Zambia
Zimbabwe

A Traveling Notebook and Chocolate Care Packages

Eighteen years old and leaving soon for Wesleyan University, Kate sat across from me during lunch last week. She was with her dad, and we were all eating coconut soup and homemade *pain au lavain* and struck up an easy conversation. Turns out Kate and three of her closest friends, who all met in kindergarten, decided to take turns writing in a notebook about their upcoming new lives and sending it through the mail, to keep in touch while away at college. "Taylor's leaving for Oregon; Aideen, Massachusetts; Kathryn, Texas," Kate told me. "And I'll be in Connecticut." Their traveling notebook will have "loose rules" and be sent via snail mail back and forth between them for the next year. "Something about seeing each other's writing and sharing it between us feels more satisfying than keeping a journal, and definitely more satisfying than Facebook—more genuine, too," Kate added.

Listening to her, I remembered when I was eighteen and leaving for college and how I now wished I'd thought to do this with some of my close friends before we all scattered to different schools. "It'll take time and care, but then we'll get to look at it later, when we're all back in San Francisco," Kate explained.

When dessert arrived, the conversation inevitably found its way to the subject of chocolate. Kate told me about the chocolate shop where she worked last year and how she used to send her friend Ellie, who was already away at college, a care package every few months with hazelnut truffles and a letter. "I hope my parents send me care packages," Kate said, glancing at her dad.

LETTER LEAD-IN

Buy a notebook and write a journal entry on the first page before sending it to a friend. Ask her to write an entry and mail it back. Include a chocolate bar and a hug.

The Places We Walk in a Day

Last year I moved downtown, so now there's no excuse why I can't get my errands done on foot. Within a few blocks, there's the postal substation where Rasco gets biscuits from Lisa and Carol and I mail my letters and parcels each week. There's a card shop, flower stand, library, market, bakery, and bookstore within five minutes of my front door. I find inspiration—even peace, when Rasco's not pulling on his leash—while out walking. Sometimes the most creative ideas happen while you're out and about on foot. There's never any traffic. Your heart rate is up. And you see and find things while walking, like that lucky penny on the sidewalk or a message tacked to a telephone pole about "Lost Bird Tiddles," all of which you'd miss if you were driving a car. Walking keeps the legs and feet strong and the spine flexible. People who sit a lot for their jobs—hello, writers—especially need to get out of their chairs and heads. Trace the outline of your foot or shoe on a separate sheet of paper. Inside recount all the places your feet have taken you over the course of a day. Invite a friend to do the same. Then find out how much of a note you can write with your feet.

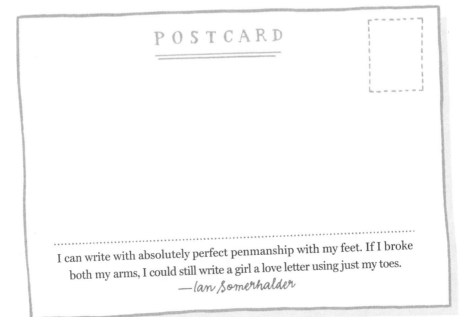

POSTCARD

I can write with absolutely perfect penmanship with my feet. If I broke both my arms, I could still write a girl a love letter using just my toes.
—Ian Somerhalder

What Makes Your Heart Swoon

Rasco and I had just returned from the vet—fleas—and were greeted by Victor, our new mail carrier. He waved as we pulled into the driveway. Four P.M. is my favorite time of day: the light on Mountain View Avenue is buttery and the small stones on the driveway sparkle from my neighbor's sprinkler spray. And, of course, it's mail delivery time. I open my metal box, peer inside, and find a letter from Glady. The envelope is addressed to me in pink ink. I delight to find Glady's careful responses to the batch of poems I'd sent her a few weeks ago.

Glady and I were members of the same writing group awhile back. We reunited at a dinner party last summer and, between courses, she leaned over and asked if I'd please send her some of my poems. When I got home, I gathered up a batch, tied them together with a piece of white ribbon, and sent them off along with a note thanking Glady for asking me.

After she typed her response, where she showed what a generous and understanding reader she is, Glady switched back to pink ink to tell me how she and her ninety-year-old boyfriend, David, were spending a few weeks in France and how she wanted to see me upon her return, to ask more questions about my poems. She closed her pink-inked portion of her letter by reminding me to "Take care, Lovey." Glady, who makes it a practice to look for and find the best in everyone she meets, calls all her friends "Lovey," which makes my heart swoon.

LETTER LEAD-IN

Go out of your way and ask someone to read something they've taken time and care to write—a poem or story—not to offer a critique but to get closer to this person's heart. Ask him to send it to you, then type your response to let him know what you genuinely appreciated. Express what made *your* heart swoon. Come on, Lovey, you know you want to.

The James Farley Post Office

The James A. Farley Post Office Building is located in New York City across the street from Penn Station. It includes services like Operation Santa, a program that began in 1912 and authorizes postmasters to respond to children's letters to Santa Claus. This also happens to be the post office where Santa's mail for the movie *Miracle on 34th Street* was sent. Until 2009, the James A. Farley Post Office was the only post office in New York City—perhaps in the entire country—to stay open to the public twenty-four hours a day, seven days a week, supporting the Postal Service's unofficial creed: Neither snow nor rain nor heat nor gloom of night stays these couriers from the swift completion of their appointed rounds.

The building's ceilings are paneled in gold, and the individual booths where you stand to purchase stamps and mail parcels are old-timey and look like they're from another century. One of the most amazing parts of the building, though, is hidden in the basement—not that I've been down there, but I've read about it. This is where a system of two-foot-wide tubes once connected the *entire* city of New York to other postal hubs and transported mail from one station to another underground. These "pneumatic mail tubes" could actually shoot hundred-pound mailbags at rates of thirty to ninety miles per hour. Rumor has it that once a live cat was even sent through the system—not something Clive approves of, by the way—and that more than one pastrami sandwich and pickle were sent from the post office nearest the Second Avenue Deli. Off the main gallery, there's a small museum of mail-related objects in glass cases. Among the items on display are mail inspection patches, advertisements for the Pony Post, a leather carrier mail pouch, and the lyrics to a song called "Mail Man Blues."

WHAT DO YOU MISS?

"You can never love people as much as you miss them," John Green wrote in his young adult novel, *An Abundance of Katherines.*

It had been a long year of people coming and going and dying. First my beloved Sicilian grandmother, Nana, passed away. As a child, I used to walk to her house after school where she greeted me at the front door with a hug, exclaiming, "Come in, Sweetie Angel." When Nana turned eighty-five, she moved to a senior center a few blocks from my house in Mill Valley and for the next ten years, my son got to visit her when he got home from school, too.

After Nana, it was Joan's turn to go. Joan was one of my closest and most trusted friends. At ninety-five, Joan was diagnosed with cancer. A few weeks before she passed away, she told me she wanted to apologize for the timing of it all, given how my nana had recently gone. Joan was like that, always thinking of how something—even her imminent death—was going to affect her closest friends. Then my husband and I decided to divorce and proceeded to sell our house (yet another death). Soon after, another friend passed away, and—well, grief can wreak havoc on a body. I lost count of the sleepless nights and grew unsteady, the needle of my inner compass no longer able to find its magnetic pole. I heard it described as the cue ball of grief effect. Pieces of my heart scattered in all directions.

So when my good pal Albert asked if I wanted to attend the Associated Writing Program Conference in Seattle with him, hinting it was time to find a way to celebrate life again by saying yes to friends' invitations, I agreed. Albert and Lynn; my sister, Ali; my friends Tammara and Jane and Courtney had all helped me pull myself back together. And of course there was Collin and cat Clive (and soon Rasco Roon) who called me back to my heart.

I booked my flight, stocked the refrigerator, left far too many reminder notes, dropped Collin and his friend Sam off at school, and caught the shuttle to SFO on a rainy Wednesday morning, where I boarded a plane bound for sunny Seattle.

When I finally reached the convention center, there was Albert's smiling face. We laughed, put on our official red laminated necklace badges, and got to work setting up our booth. We strategized our plan: we'd make every meal count (check); we'd gather 500+ names and e-mail addresses from conference attendees for our "lists" (check); we'd talk up each other's books and accomplishments (check); we'd take turns roaming the convention hall and attend a few panels (check). When it was my turn to roam, I wandered over to the *FIELD Magazine* booth. "What do you miss?" the woman sitting behind a table covered with postcards greeted me. "If you only knew," I thought. She handed me a postcard and invited me to answer the question in 140 characters and then pop it in the mail to enter their What I Miss contest. I told her, "I can do that."

LETTER LEAD-IN

In 140 characters, whittle down who or what *you* miss. "I miss a lot of things," I wanted to say to that woman, "how my nana smelled of lemons and roses, the soups Joan made, my house by the creek, how my son would sit on my lap after school and rest his hands on my face."

Dear Reader,

Letters carry the intimacy and texture of everyday life. In the space of a letter there is room for thought and feeling, news of the emotional weather, the possibility of writing one's way into a clearer understanding. Brain and heart and hand. Bits of decoration and verbal flourish. Letters hold time—they aren't necessarily instant. Sometimes they are written (and occasionally read) over a week or two; the conversation can last for years.

I enjoy the task of addressing envelopes. Writing out someone's name becomes a calligraphy of friendship. Being an artist I am drawn to the circles, triangles, and squares that actual letters make, the shapes of the words on the page. The letter L so clean and straight in print becomes looping and flowing in cursive. I love that we use the word *letter* to describe the 26 symbols of the alphabet and the plural *letters* to describe our correspondence; *literature*, our knowledge of letters.

At this point in my life I find myself increasingly writing the hardest notes of all—the grief notes where the silences are immense and the words very small.

With joy in your creative endeavors,

J. Ruth Gendler

A SAMPLE OF J. RUTH GENDLER'S WRITING
From *The Book of Qualities*

IMAGINATION

When Imagination walks, she writes letters to the earth. When she runs, her feet trace postcards to the sun. And when she dances, when she dances, she sends love letters to the stars. Some people accuse Imagination of being a liar. They don't understand that she has her own ways of uncovering the truth. She studied journalism in junior high school. It gave her an excuse to leave school early and interview interesting people. She was surprisingly good at writing articles. When in doubt, she just made things up. More recently, Imagination has been working as a fortuneteller in the circus. She has this way of telling your fortune so clearly that you believe her, and then your wishes start to come true.

J. RUTH GENDLER is a painter, printmaker, and the author of three books of lyrical nonfiction: *Notes on the Need for Beauty, Changing Light*, and the long-time best-seller *The Book of Qualities*. She is both a student and a teacher of the creative process and can be reached virtually at http://ruthgendlerstudio.com.

DEAR LIFE

I've taught poetry workshops with California Poets in the Schools in hundreds of classrooms in public and private schools over the years, where the teachers are welcoming and many are eager to sit and create poems right along with their students. To some of these teachers, I attribute rock-star status. One of them is Ann Marie Padilla, at Tamalpais Valley Elementary School. Ms. Padilla has a winning teaching style. Children—my son included, when he won the lottery and was placed in her fourth-grade classroom—blossom under her guidance. She is kind, good-humored, and calm, and she has a knack for instilling confidence in her students so that they, too, believe they have something important inside of them to write about. And, of course, they do. Ms. Padilla lights fires of inspiration in young minds and hearts, joins her students at their writing tables, and asks insightful questions of the visiting poet so everyone can better understand how to let their imaginations lead them toward uncovering the truth of their inner treasure. Her students trust her and take great risks while writing because of her.

Last fall, one of Ms. Padilla's shyest students—I'll call her A.—was having a challenging time with a few of the girls in class who were excluding her. A. wrote a poem called "Dear Life" that made me and Ms. P. exchange that certain look when a student takes a risk and shares something that is true and heartbreakingly beautiful:

Dear Life,
Remember beneath the river where the fire flashes so close it feels like
    love?
Then comes a cold wind and you feel like you're invisible?
Dear Life, everything is silent. The sun stands up, easy to reach
and I just finish wrapping myself around my heart.
—A.

HANDLE WITH CARE

Write a note or short letter that begins "Dear Life." Say on the page what you can't say out loud when you're pretending everything's okay, because we all know sometimes it's not. Find a teacher like Ms. Padilla to read or send it to.

WHEN CAUGHT IN THE DRAMA OF YOUR OWN LIFE

Sometimes I can get so involved in the drama of my own life's orbit—the sun, moon, and stars of all my worries and concerns—that I forget to inquire about the dramas and comedies of my friends' orbits. On a trajectory of my own making, I forget to slow down and gather my thoughts back into the present moment, where the best and only real presents (presence) reside. Once I went nearly a year without writing a single letter to a single friend. How lame is that? Somehow I forgot how much contentment there is in putting the kettle on for tea and picking up my pen to escape into composing a letter. The author of *Griffin & Sabine*, Nick Bantock, says, "Letter writing is an excellent way of slowing down this lunatic helter-skelter universe long enough to gather one's thoughts." Yes, indeed!

Find some cozy place to rest within your orbit (see suggestions on page 121) and write a single page to a friend you have forgotten about for a while. You know the one. Use the top half of the paper to ask questions you genuinely want your friend's response to. Use the bottom half to let your friend know what you've been up to, why it's been so long between letters.

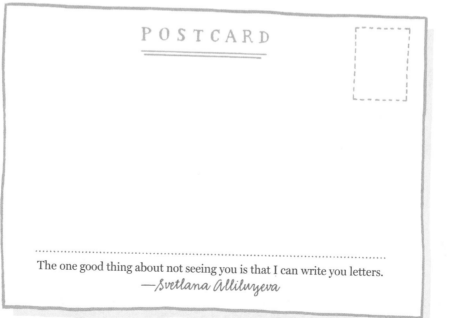

POSTCARD

The one good thing about not seeing you is that I can write you letters.
—*Svetlana Alliluyeva*

Meet Us at the Creek

Late in the day, my son and I are on the floor of our summer rental in Ashland, Oregon, building a house of cards. Slick red-numbered rooms slip from our hands as I attempt to explain how his dad and I care about each other, even if we argue over how to divide up a slice of time. "Dad wants to read, so how about you and I take a walk?" I suggest. Collin shuffles the deck, shrugs, looks away. Finally he gets up to find a pen, writes something on a piece of paper, folds it into an airplane, and floats it across the room. After some hang time, it lands in his father's lap. His dad looks up, his expression pained as though asking us to *please, just go.* I grab my sunglasses while Collin finds his backpack. And soon we're off, making up songs about piled-up rocks and tiny fish that dart between our feet, all desire of wanting life to somehow be different vanishing behind us. We talk about the comedy we'll see tomorrow, plan where to go for dinner, discuss what flavor we'll order at Zoey's Ice Cream Shop for dessert. Collin tells me how he wishes summer didn't have to end. We continue upstream, making a game of jumping from boulder to boulder until there, up ahead, standing on a splintered bridge, Owen waves. "Hey, Dad, watch!" Collin yells and picks up a stone, skipping it three times. Minnows scatter and my heart collapses into the depths of this moment, into what matters most.

LETTER LEAD-IN

My stumble and splash and Collin's boyish laugh were what mattered most that afternoon in Ashland. What matters most to you today? Write a note or sail a paper airplane to someone to share your feelings. Even if it's just where you want to go play or meet later for dinner.

An Alternate Ending

Middle of October, a month before our divorce, Owen and I were in New York City, walking through Central Park, talking about how I hurt him, how he hurt me. It was an old story. I suggested that perhaps we could find a way to change this and invited him to sit on a bench and write a new ending. To his credit, he did. I pulled out my notebook and he found a pen. With a sweep of my hand, I asked him to write down everything I'd ever said or left unsaid that he needed to hear me say or restate. I asked if I could do the same. We actively looked for, so then found, evidence for each other's best traits. Pretty soon, Time's dark wings no longer covered up the fear of what we thought we each had to protect. The head settled back and let the heart lead again. We acknowledged our respect for the other's sensitivities (and idiosyncracies). We agreed that we both adored the same freckle-faced boy and perhaps that was more than enough. While a cold wind cleared the sky clean of clouds, we walked to a café, ordered tea, shared a plate of cookies. I told him I no longer wanted to play the same old game of sabotage, so he folded up the board, and I put each token away.

LETTER LEAD-IN

When you and a friend or partner are having a tough time, sometimes it helps to switch it up, take a little trip, and rewrite the way you usually do things. Literally take out pen and paper and make a new list, script, story. Who do you want to stop playing the same old game with? What new ending or new beginning will you each write?

Start with Where You're Living

During my twenties, I lived in a studio apartment on the second floor of a blue building on Grattan Street, in San Francisco's hip Cole Valley neighborhood. The closet was bigger than the bathroom, so Tammara suggested I turn it into an office. There was also a small deck; "Kares, that's a fire escape," my sister said, when she came to visit. No matter. In the kitchen, a window looked onto a large pittosporum tree. In the center of the living room/bedroom/dining room was a loft bed that I'd hired a carpenter to build bookshelves around so my elevated space could double as a desk. Did I mention the studio was located across the street from a fire station? (It was.) No matter. I made friends with the siren sounds by putting them into my stories. Depending on where you live, it helps to have a vivid imagination. From Lynn's apartment, you could hear the generators on the UCSF campus, so we decided that they sounded like waves crashing on a beach. Soothing.

During the day, I worked at an art gallery, answering phones: "Hello, Joanne Chappell Gallery," and took orders from five art consultants who were sometimes friendly, sometimes not. In the evenings, I sat zazen at the San Francisco Zen Center, then walked up to Lone Mountain campus at the University of San Francisco, where I attended graduate school.

Come spring, when sirens started showing up in my dreams *and* in my poems, I signed up for a writing retreat at a monastery in the Carmel Valley, headed by a teacher I'd been wanting to study with. Early on a Friday, I drove my Honda Civic down the peninsula, then continued along a narrow, unpaved road, thanking my grandparents the entire way for buying me a car with four-wheel drive. Arriving at Tassajara, I immediately fell in love with the pebbled paths, my cabin, the sound of the creek, and a blue-eyed man in a hat, who was studying a map on the side of the office wall. "Do you know where the yurt is?" he asked. That's where we walked to meet Natalie Goldberg, the author of *Writing Down the Bones.*

Natalie greeted us all that June morning by asking if we'd introduce ourselves with the name of the city where we were born and where we were living now. She explained that she liked imagining the trajectory of how people move through the world. I was shy that week, but my mind was wild. The whole world kept swooping through me just like the shadows of the blue jays that kept me company while I'd write. On the next to last day, I decided to be brave and share something I'd written. The assignment: to use the phrase "What I really want to say is" any time we started drifting into writing that was muddy and safe. Reading out loud, having Natalie and the others in the workshop hear me, changed the way I felt about myself as a writer. I returned home to San Francisco to discover my entire life had opened into a wider neighborhood of love, appreciation, and wonder. I even found more ways to incorporate the sounds of sirens into my poems, letters, stories.

LETTER LEAD-IN

What have you done—what *would* you do—for yourself that's entirely new, possibly even life-changing? If it hasn't happened yet, what would it be? Write someone a letter, sharing this story. As you write, toss in, "But what I really want to say is . . ." Write it on the back of a map and end your letter with a homemade heart.

Dear Reader,

You can use a computer, but I always say you should be able to write with a pen, because someday your computer might break, or you might not have access to electricity. It's sort of like driving: you still have to know how to walk. I consider writing an athletic activity: the more you practice, the better you get at it. The reason you keep your hand moving is because there's often a conflict between the editor and the creator. The editor is always on our shoulder saying, "Oh, you shouldn't write that. It's no good." But when you have to keep the hand moving, it's an opportunity for the creator to have a say. All the other rules of writing practice support that primary rule of keeping your hand moving. The goal is to allow the written word to connect with your original mind, to write down the first thought you flash on, before the second and third thoughts come in . . . I call that place "wild mind." Wild mind isn't just your mind; it's the whole world moving through you. With it, you give voice to a very large life, even though you might only be talking about your grandmother's closet with its particular wallpaper and floor. It's an awareness of everything through one thing. Love,

natalie

A SAMPLE OF NATALIE GOLDBERG'S WRITING

I WANT TO SAY

Before I'm lost to time and the midwest
I want to say I was here
I loved the half light all winter
I want you to know before I leave
that I liked the towns living along the back of the Mississippi

I loved the large heron filling the sky
the slender white egret at the edge of the shore
I came to love my life here
fell in love with the color grey
the unending turn of seasons

Let me say
I loved Hill City
the bench in front of the tavern
the small hill to the lake
I loved the morning frost on the bell in New Albin
and the money I made as a poet
I was thankful for the white night
the sky of so many wet summers
Before I leave this whole world of my friends
I want to tell you I loved the rain on large store windows
had more croissants here in Minneapolis
than the French do in Lyons
I read the poets of the midwest
their hard crusts of bread dark goat cheese
and was nourished not hungry where they lived
I ate at the edges of state lines and boundaries

Know I loved the cold the tap of bare branches against windows
know there will not be your peonies in spring
wherever I go
the electric petunias
and your orange zinnias

NATALIE GOLDBERG blends her Zen practice with her art and her teachings, encouraging people from around the world to fall in love with their lives through creativity. She's the author of nine books, including *Writing Down the Bones: Freeing the Writer Within,* which has sold more than one million copies and been translated into fourteen languages. She lives in northern New Mexico.

YOUR MOST IMPORTANT QUESTION

Joan and I met in the Berkeley Hills, at the home of a mutual friend. Though fifty years separated us by age, our friendship sparked joy from the instant we began chatting at the buffet table and didn't care a whit about what decade or country we were each born into.

Soon after that birthday party, Joan and I began to exchange letters. Heart offerings and advice, mixed in with news of our lives. Joan's husband, Art, had died a few months before our meeting, and she was beginning a collection of linked essays on aging and matters of the heart. After a few exchanged letters, she called to ask if she could hire me as her editor. For the next fifteen years, between snail-mail sent letters, we met every few months at her dining room table for work meetings and lunch. It was over Joan's homemade soups and our favorite Cheeseboard Pizzas that we'd discuss the progress of her manuscript, *A Different Woman: The View from Ninety.* I learned a lot about love and loss and taking risks from my dear friend and confidant, Joan Hill Kip, during those lunch meetings. She became among my closest friends.

Just after Joan turned ninety-five, she was diagnosed with cancer and we accelerated plans for her book to be published. Many of her essays had already found homes in literary magazines, and one had won an award in a national writing competition judged by Phillip Lopate. On our next-to-last visit, Joan showed me the essay she was completing—she wrote until the end—titled "Watching Myself Disappear." She asked my opinion as to whether I thought it was alright to begin her essay with a letter she had written to her great-nephew, Kip, her namesake, who had just turned five. "But isn't that breaking some rule, Karin?" she asked in her British accent. (I loved that I was always called Karin.) I explained to Joan that there were no rules anymore, especially since she had reached the level of writing from her heart's truest center. There wasn't time in our relationship to be anything less than utterly honest with each other. Here's the question and Joan's answer, in the form of that letter she penned to her beloved great-nephew.

Dear Kip,

I hear that you looked at some pictures of mummies and got to wondering what it would be like to "become bones." And then, you thought about me, whose bones are especially ancient. I love that your thoughts drift across 3,000 miles from your house in Connecticut to my house in California. You ask if I'm afraid of becoming bones—if I'm scared. That's an important question. My answer is No. Each age is a new adventure, isn't it? The only difference is that you know where you are going—like one of these days into first grade—whereas I don't know. I can only dream about where I'm going. And this makes it more exciting. Write me again if you have more questions, since I love questions and I love you.

—Aunt Joan

LETTER LEAD-IN

Wonder out loud about your most pressing question or most unbearable fear and then write to someone older and wiser and ask her if she might share her thoughts on the subject. If you're lucky, your answer will be something a five-year-old can understand.

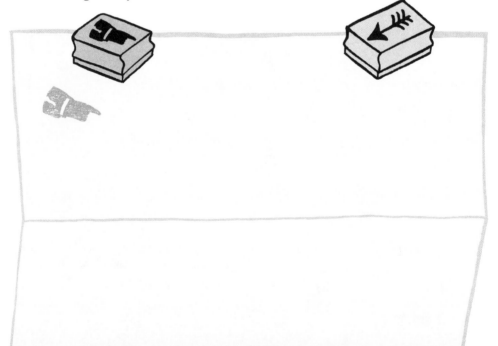

Start and End Inside the Parentheses

My English teachers always advised, "You can break the rules once you know the rules." But sometimes we have to break the rules even before we know them. The rules of sentence structure, that is. Even if you don't know the rules today, give yourself permission to play and engage with this prompt and write exactly what you would put into the parentheses, right from the beginning. Yes, your entire note or letter can be *inside* the parentheses. Sometimes we put our heart words, the deepest and most emotional parts of our writing, inside the parentheses. That's precisely where our gold can be found and shared.

Today, begin a letter with that one bookend of a hug—the opening parenthesis—and continue to write straight from the heart, not bothering with punctuation or sentence structure, and definitely not waiting until you get to the middle of your letter to include something you love about someone or saving the word *love* until the sign-off at the end. Break some rules. Write what you feel from the very start. (You can also just write and write to your heart's content. . .)

POSTCARD

I hold that the parentheses are by far the most important parts of a non-business letter. —*D. H. Lawrence*

Dear Reader,

After reading Richard Hugo's book *31 Letters and 13 Dreams*, I wrote a
letter-poem back to him in answer—I couldn't not. Hugo had been dead
twelve years by then, but one of the gifts of both poems and letters is
that you can speak to anyone in them and through them. You can send
words into the world in ways that matter even when they can't be directly
received. You can write to the living and to the dead. You can write to
other people, to animals, to history, to objects, to your own sadness,
exhilaration, or confusion. You can write to the past and to the future. And
whoever the poem or letter is addressed to, we are always also writing to
ourselves, thinking and feeling through, by and with words, our own lives.

   We can't compose our outer lives—but in composing a letter or poem,
you can alter the inner world, revise it, and, within that deeper looking,
you can change who you are. And invite someone else to join you in that
changed existence, and be changed again in turn when they respond.
XXX

—*Jane*

A SAMPLE OF JANE HIRSHFIELD'S WRITING

LETTER TO HUGO FROM LATER

Dear Dick: In order to xerox your book I had to break
the spine. Somehow that felt right, because to get
the life of anything it seems you have to let some part
be broken. Here, now, it is spring. It must be there
as well, if you can see it. And the poppies are
stringing themselves out the way they do in California,
and the Indian Paintbrush dabbing itself in. Also,

the horses are sick with strangles. That's true, although
I also think you'd like the way the word leaps out,
the way the lump does also under the jaw of the sick ones,
making your stomach fall. And maybe I say it too because
it's hard to speak the rest until you've loosed what sticks
in the throat. Watching a small white moth as it goes stitching
across the trees—that helps as well. The particular does.
I envy the way you managed to pack so many parts of the world
in such a little space, the way you'd go from pouring a glass
of beer to something American and huge. I don't write much
about America, or even people. For you, people were what there was:
you talked with and about them and stayed up late
to love those high-lobbed lives. I'd often enough rather
talk to horses. I lived not far from you that summer the book
came out—in Lolo. I knew you were in town, but never thought
to knock or ask to join a class. I wonder what might have happened,
if I'd have come to love the barrooms more, the haze of smoke
and talking. I was young and might have. I'm planning to give
your poem to a workshop in Kansas City, along with Horace
     and Komachi
and maybe this one if I'm feeling brave. I bet you'd like to know
the book sells higher now than when it was first published.
And like knowing it's still cheap: five bucks, a bargain.
Poems shouldn't cost a lot, we'd both agree, except for how
the spine breaks when you try to pin them down. It hurts but not
too much, and anyhow, one thing no poet does is look away.
And now you're past it. You wrote: *I want my life inside to go on
as long as I do*, and it did. The big fish are almost gone now
from the places you once went to, but clean or dirty, water keeps on
pouring. Today I bait the hook with you, as you did with Denise
and Jim and Gary. We throw each other in and hope the line bends.
I'm sorry to have pulled up such a small one—I'll throw it back, I
promise, while it's still alive and able to swim on. I'm sorry too

I missed you in this life, and send you blessings. Please do what you can for the horses. Your tardy friend.

J.

JANE HIRSHFIELD has two new books coming out in 2015: *The Beauty* (poems) and *Ten Windows: How Great Poems Transform the World* (essays). A chancellor of the Academy of American Poets, Hirshfield has received many prizes and awards, including fellowships from the Guggenheim and Rockefeller foundations and the National Endowment for the Arts. Her work appears frequently in *The New Yorker* and on Garrison Keillor's *Writer's Almanac*.

FAR FROM HOME

I hatched a plan to travel through Greece with my cousin Dawnie the summer after my twenty-third birthday. The first part of our trip started with catching up on much-needed sleep, so we snoozed our way across Santorini's beaches. Next stop was the Pindus Mountains in northern Greece, where we met up with a group of professional trekkers who inspired us to hike fifteen miles a day for two weeks. Break out the moleskin! Our summer adventures nearly ended though on Crete when we ran out of money. Luckily, because we're resourceful and didn't want to go home yet, we found jobs renting sea kayaks and cleaning hotel rooms in the small village of Loutro. Here, we met new friends, bartered to eat at the local taverna, and celebrated Dawnie's twenty-second birthday before taking a tour of nearby Naxos.

It was on Naxos that I found myself hiking alone one afternoon, after my cousin rode off on the back of a motorcycle with a young Greek man named Demetris. Halfway up the side of a hill, I wandered into a grassy meadow and found a herd of grazing sheep. Amazed at my good fortune, I remembered something from childhood about animals and how they made me feel more alive. The grass filled the distance between their grazing and my boots; the mountain was covered with small white stones. With each heartbeat, I wanted to step closer yet didn't want to scare them. So I sat right down in the middle of that meadow rimmed with olive trees, among those chewing woolly beings, slipped a pen and notepad from my backpack, and began to write a letter. Not knowing who to write to, I wrote to my own timid heart, thanking her for bringing me to Greece, where she could remember and retrieve something true and important about herself.

LETTER LEAD-IN

What letter would you write to your heart? What friend would you share your heart letter with? "Alone in that meadow, I sat until I knew I was happy, in fine company, sunlight pouring through everything: rocks, sheep, trees, even me. —K."

YOUR LIFELINES

Is there a poem or a passage from a novel that you keep with you as a life-line? Are you a fan of underlining passages as a reminder to yourself: "Yes, return to this!" I return to the words of Marion Winik who, among her books, columns, and NPR commentaries, wrote *Rules for the Unruly*, a portion of which I found written on a refrigerator magnet! In seven short lifeline sentences, see if anything Ms. Winik wrote keeps you afloat too.

1. The path is not straight. 2. Mistakes need not be fatal. 3. People are more important than achievements or possessions. 4. Be gentle with your parents. 5. Never stop doing what you most care about. 6. Learn to use a semicolon. 7. You will find love.

Is there an author whose work you particularly care about who acts as your lifeline? If you can't find a direct e-mail or mailing address for a specific poet or author, try getting in touch with her publisher. The gesture of writing a letter can bring you closer to her work.

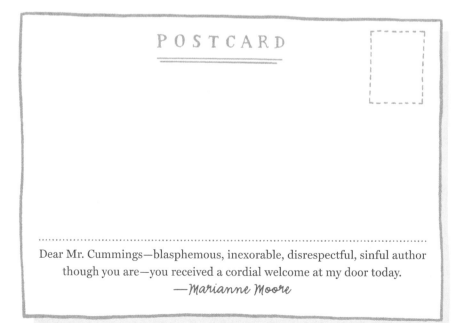

POSTCARD

Dear Mr. Cummings—blasphemous, inexorable, disrespectful, sinful author though you are—you received a cordial welcome at my door today.
—*Marianne Moore*

WRITTEN WITH ABANDON

Have you ever been tempted to read someone else's mail? Have you ever succumbed to that temptation, reading fast, afraid you'll be caught peaking at something you aren't supposed to see (and later wished you hadn't)? Or maybe you walked away from temptation, happier for your resolve. Writer David Sedaris says: "If you read someone else's diary, you get what you deserve." The fact is that even when we go to great lengths to keep our writing private, it might still be read. We can't live in fear of censorship. It's important to write with abandon sometimes—without worrying about who might read our words—to familiarize ourselves and make friends with what's piled up in the closets of our mind. This kind of writing isn't anything you have to share with anyone. In fact, after you write, you may decide to rip the pages into tiny pieces or crumple them up to use as kindling for a bonfire. Before you rip or burn something you've written, though, see if there's a small section—the size that fits on the back of a postcard, say—that you'd be willing to share with a friend. Maybe recopy it or stuff it in an envelope, along with the rest of your "letter" in the form of envelope confetti.

P O S T C A R D

I write letters to you that you'll never see. —*Jennifer Elisabeth*

A Letter Never Sent

My grandfather, Allen Evert Nelson III, whom I called Papa, taught me about hard work, generosity, and abundance. Though I'm sure I thanked him over the years for paying for dance lessons, footing the bill for my education, taking me and my sister on lavish summer vacations, and buying my first-ever new car, I don't know if I ever had the right words or maturity to thank him properly, in a letter, for teaching me about the connected feelings of generosity and abundance.

I think of him this morning, as I stand at the stove making breakfast. He and his younger brother (Uncle Bob) were often hungry, so I take my time making one of Papa's favorite meals, scrambled eggs. I am grateful for the choice my son has between waffles or pancakes; apricot or raspberry jam. Before we leave the house for school, I sit on the bench in the mudroom and look at the shoe hutch, filled to capacity. Papa had to go to work at a young age, selling newspapers in front of the Ferry Building in San Francisco to support himself. Many years later, when one of his business ventures took off, he indulged in what he never had when he was young: new shoes. Papa understood about being creative—and generous—rather than competitive when it came to making money. While he was making his fortune and certainly afterward, he supported friends and family members in achieving their dreams, so they could help themselves make their marks too. Nearly a quarter of a century has passed since Papa left the planet, yet what he taught me has grown stronger.

Light fades. We navigate the end of another summer. Driving back from the beach, the young man sitting in the passenger seat who my grandfather never knew sings along to the radio. I count horses grazing the August hills and watch lights twinkle beyond the Bay, where Papa worked long days when he was my son's age. I hold appreciation for how many blessings and choices I have now, because of him. "Don't say a word," I beg my heart, not wanting even love to interfere with this much gratitude.

LETTER LEAD-IN

Don't wait until someone has died to send that person a letter.
Say everything now that you always meant to express.

DEFINITION OF A POSTSCRIPT

P.S. stands for postscript. You add a P.S. to the end of a note or letter when you want to include additional information. Or you might add a P.S. when you get to the end of your letter and (oh, no) see that you accidentally left something out of what you wrote. You really don't want to squish it into the body of your letter or note, so you tack it on below with that handy abbreviated P.S. Sometimes I even write my P.S. as "Post Script," just because I can.

Your P.S. may be something that enlivens your letter's meaning. It might be a joke you want to add. It might be a P.S. to flirt a little or tell on yourself or extend a last-minute invitation. And then there's always the P.P.S., which comes in handy when you've left something out of your P.S. Well, you get the picture.

P.S. Think of this book as a long letter I've written to *you*. (It is!) Now it's your turn . . .

Instructions for Making an Envelope

You can create a template for making an envelope by deconstructing (aka gently pulling open) a commercially made envelope and using it as a pattern to trace and cut out from a piece of paper, a map, a page from an old book, a grocery bag, or a page of newspaper. Or you could print out Lindsey Bugbee's handy envelope template. Lindsey likes using upcycled materials and is the founder of The Postman's Knock, a calligraphy and graphic design company based in Boulder, Colorado. Here's a breakdown of Lindsey's four-step process:

1. Trace around the template (opened-up envelope).
2. Cut it out.
3. Fold the bottom up.
4. Fold the sides in.

While you have the sides folded in, trace around them on the bottom so you'll know where to put the glue or tape. Fold the sides in on some small dots of glue or "tape pillows." You can glue a small square of light-colored paper on the front of your homemade envelope so you'll have a place to write the recipient's name, street address, city, state, and zip code.

Acknowledgments

My thanks to my agent, Stefanie von Borstel, for encouraging me to sit down and get my book proposals written, and to Jennifer Urban-Brown, a wonder of an editor, for her handwritten notes and inspiring lunches in New York City.

For radical hospitality and for putting a roof over my head while I gathered material for this book, eight bows to Tassajara Zen Mountain Monastery, Hale Pili Aloha ("House of Close Friends"), Buck's Cabin, The Mill Valley Public Library, Poets House, and The Writers' Nest on Mountain View Avenue.

For their time and generosity in answering my e-mail requests, my appreciation to Natalie Goldberg, Wendy Mass, Ava Dellaira, Neil Gaiman, Christine DiCrocco, Ruth Ozeki, Norman Fischer, Lucille Lang Day, J. Ruth Gendler, Claire Dederer, Gary Snyder, Jon J Muth, Allen Spiegel, Albert Flynn DeSilver, Sam Hamill, Alison Luterman, and especially Jane Hirshfield for continuing to pave the way.

For friendly copyediting assistance, thank you, Julia Gaviria; for art design, thank you, Daniel Urban-Brown, Allison Meierding, and Joy Gosney; and for publicity help, thank you, Kate Levy and Steven Pomije. For care and assistance along the way, my love to Megan Freeman; Maria Nemeth; Albert Flynn DeSilver; Lynn Mundell; Marlene Benke; Brian Lewis; Alison and Brad Altmann; Barbara Rounds; Leslie Berkler; Sean Perry; Mary Lea Crawley; Dawn, Matt, and Luc Antonelli; Don, Bette, and Owen Prell; Nina and Allen Nelson; Joan Kip; Leslie James; Mike Epley; Sandy Diamond; Prartho Sereno; Courtney, Marco, Nicholas, and Sebi della Cava; Kathy Evans; Carolyn Ingram; Ryan Ali; Dana Dworin; Fran Katz; Susan Williams; Christy Brown; Tammara Norman; Anna and Edwin Hamilton; Bryce Brownlie; Eden Clearbrook; Russ Mitchell; Claire Blotter; Terry Glass; Eldon Beck; Rod Septka; James Higgins; Meg and Jeremy Levie; Julie Westcott; Bob and Karen Kustel; Kristin Laymon;

Mark Grothman; Travis Woods; Ron Shoop; Jane Flint; Cynthia Shraeger; Lyn Follett; Braeda Horan; Sasha Faulkner; Katie MacBride; Glady Thatcher; Anne Barrows; Diana and Craig Parker; Michael Williams; Peter Barnes; Pooneh Yamini; Barbara Renton; Nancy Malloy; and Francois Levenier.

My appreciation to independent bookstore owners and staff, with a special nod to The Depot and Book Passage Bookstore for creating welcoming and inspiring spaces to shop, buy, and talk books; the creative teams at Roost Books, Shambhala Publications, and Penguin Random House; the intrepid souls in the California Poets in the Schools program; and all the dedicated classroom teachers in the United States, Canada, and Australia who use and recommend my books to their students—and the students who recommend them to their teachers.

A rub behind the ears to Clive and Rasco Roon for reminding me of the sanity of naps and for leading me away from my desk for walks. And always an extra hug to Collin Prell, muse-of-the-heart, for making every day my lucky day.

Books + an Article That Inspired *Write Back Soon*!

Bantock, Nick. *Griffin & Sabine*.

Burke, Kathryn. *Letter Writing in America*.

Campbell, Jen. *Weird Things Customers Say in Bookstores*.

Day, Lucille Lang. *The Curvature of Blue*.

Dederer, Claire. *Poser: My Life in Twenty-Three Yoga Poses*.

Dellaira, Ava. *Love Letters to the Dead*.

DeSilver, Albert Flynn. *Letters to Early Street*.

Diamond, Sandy. *Bliss, Danger & Gods: Quotes of Risk & Passion*.

Fischer, Norman. *Training in Compassion: Zen Teachings on the Practice of Lojong*.

Goldberg, Natalie. *Writing Down the Bones: Freeing the Writer Within*.

Hegarty, John. *Hegarty on Creativity: There Are No Rules*.

Hirshfield, Jane. *The Lives of the Heart*.

Issa, Kobayashi. *The Spring of My Life and Selected Haiku*, translated by Sam Hamill.

Kalman, Maira. *My Favorite Things*.

Keenan, Marina. *The Opposite of Loneliness*.

Kleon, Austin. *Show Your Work*.

———. *Steal Like an Artist*.

Leedy, Loreen. *Messages in the Mailbox*.

Luterman, Alison. *Various Poems and Essays from* The Sun *Magazine*.

Muth, Jon J. *Zen Shorts*.

Neumeyer, Peter F., ed. *Floating Worlds: The Letters of Edward Gorey & Peter F. Neumeyer*.

Ono, Yoko. *Acorn*.

Ozeki, Ruth. *A Tale for the Time Being*.

"A Point of View: Mourning the Loss of the Written Word." *BBC News Magazine*. www.bbc.co.uk/news/magazine-16871715. February 3, 2012.

Sankovitch, Nina. *Signed, Sealed, Delivered: Celebrating the Joys of Letter Writing.*

Smith, Keri. *Everything Is Connected: Reimagining the World One Postcard at a Time.*

Stafford, William, and Marvin Bell. *Segues: A Correspondence in Poetry.*

Vry, Silke. *Paul Klee for Children.*

Winfrey, Oprah. *What I Know for Sure.*

Wriglesworth, Chad, ed. *Distant Neighbors: The Selected Letters of Wendell Berry and Gary Snyder.*

Index of Exercises

A NOTE PASSED TO YOU FROM:

POSTCARD-SIZED PROMPT

SPECIAL DELIVERY

Credits

A Note Passed to You from Gary Snyder © Gary Snyder. Used by permission of the author.

Letter from *Distant Neighbors: The Selected Letters of Wendell Berry and Gary Snyder.* Copyright © 2014 by Chad Wriglesworth. Reprinted by permission of Counterpoint.

A Note Passed to You from Neil Gaiman is based on advice given in two different interviews: one with Chris Hardwick from the *Nerdist* podcast on July 12, 2011, and one with John O'Connell for *Time Out* on October 5, 2006. Copyright © 2015 by Neil Gaiman; used by permission.

A Note Passed to You from Wendy Mass © Wendy Mass. Used by permission of the author.

A Note Passed to You from Albert Flynn DeSilver © Albert Flynn DeSilver. Used by permission of the author.

A Note Passed to You from Jon J Muth © Jon J Muth. Used by permission of the author.

Excerpt from *Zen Shorts* by Jon J Muth. Scholastic Inc./Scholastic Press. Copyright © 2005 by Jon J Muth. Reprinted by permission.

A Note Passed to You from Alison Luterman © Alison Luterman. Used by permission of the author.

Excerpt from "The Secret of My Success" by Alison Luterman. Copyright © 2003 by Alison Luterman. Published in 2003 by *The Sun*. Reprinted by permission of the author.

A Note Passed to You from Ava Dellaira © Ava Dellaira. Used by permission of the author.

About the Author

KAREN BENKE is the author of a poetry collection, *Sister* (Conflux Press, 2004), and two popular books on creative writing adventures—*Rip the Page!* (Roost Books, 2010) and *Leap Write In!* (Roost Books, 2013). The recipient of grants and awards from *Poets & Writers*, the Marin Arts Council Fund for Writers, the Hedgebrook Foundation, and the Djerassi Resident Artists Program, her books have been featured in *FamilyFun Magazine*, *Marin Magazine*, *Kids Book Review* (Australia), *Children's Book Review*, and *SouleMama*. She is the creator of The Museletter, a writing mentor, a workshop leader for kids and adults, and a long-time teacher with California Poets in the Schools. She lives north of the Golden Gate Bridge with her family and prefers letters delivered to her physical mailbox, although she can be reached at her website (http://karenbenke.com).